make money
make money

make money
make money

by
Norman Cumming

edited by
Alan Haydn Griffiths

BBC Books

Published to accompany a series of television programmes
prepared in consultation with the Continuing Education
Advisory council

Published by BBC Books,
a division of BBC Enterprises Limited,
Woodlands, 80 Wood Lane, London W12 0TT
First Published 1989

ISBN 0 563 21455 4

Set in 9/12pt Cheltenham Light
by Phoenix Photosetting Ltd, Chatham
Printed and bound in Great Britain
by Fletchers of Norwich
Cover printed by Fletchers of Norwich

Contents ·

Foreword ·

Not so long ago only the rich invested, the sort of folk with posh accents that populate the upmarket soap operas on British television. No longer. Most of us have been growing steadily more prosperous since the second world war and in the 1980s the investing classes have become a clear majority.

Britain is now a society in which almost 70 per cent of families own their homes, there are more shareholders than trade union members, inheritance is reaching well down the social scale as today's middle class inherit the mortgage-paid homes of their parents, and in general, people have more money to save and invest than ever before. As a result, an increasing number are no longer content to keep their savings in the local building society, their piggy banks or in a sock under the bed. They want to become more knowledgeable about the investment opportunities available to them and more adventurous about where they put their money. This book, and the BBC Television series which it grew out of, are designed to meet their needs.

As is only fitting for a nation of home owners it begins with property, the single biggest investment most folk will ever make. It goes on to explain the merits of fixed-investment securities, from corporate bonds to government gilts, and the world of stocks and shares. It finishes with the mysteries of futures and traded options, which are not generally to be recommended for small investors, never mind widows and orphans. But then, many people who regularly scan the financial pages of the press to check on their shares would never have dreamed of owning shares a decade ago. So the next decade might well bring a host of small British investors eagerly watching the movements of pork bellies on the Chicago futures market.

This book points the way. It is for the new generation of small investors who want to raise their horizons and make their savings work harder for them. It won't replace professional financial advice; but it will help you to evaluate that advice better. It probably won't make you rich; but it offers the sort of sound guidance which should give you a better return on your savings than you are getting now, without risk to your shirt.

So enjoy it, learn from it, and prosper.

Good luck!

Andrew Neil

London   January 1989

*I*ntroduction ·

This book accompanies the BBC television series of the same name. Both have been created in response to the suspicion that many people invest in property or shares rather as they would back a racehorse. The name seems nice, the moon is in the right phase – and they feel lucky . . .

Unfortunately there are plenty of professional investors in the markets who are eating people who invest in this way for breakfast, lunch and dinner. Both the author of this book and the producer of the television series believe that it is only fair to give amateur investors some of the tools and the knowledge of their professional rivals. No one likes an unfair contest – particularly when they're consistently on the losing side.

So this book is aimed at those who have money to invest and feel themselves to be intellectually naked when it comes to investment expertise. Whereas the television programmes will give you, the investor, the uneasy feeling that there is a lot more to know about investment, this book will provide you with at least a first protective layer of financial literacy. You do not need a formal training in economics or finance to read it. We have assumed that you do not know what dividends, options, or even shares are.

The book examines the main different types of investment available in Britain today. It looks at how they've performed in the past, and tries to explain how professionals in the investment business look at the different markets in their efforts to predict what's going to happen in the future.

Above all, the book gives practical advice with the aim of helping you to make better investment decisions. When you have finished, you should have some idea of what makes the main investment markets tick; you should get more from reading the financial pages of newspapers; above all, you should be in a better position to make money make money.

What's here

The book covers the British property, shares, fixed interest, and futures and options markets. The property section focuses on residential property – houses and flats – although it also looks very briefly at larger-scale commercial property investment.

Private investors have rediscovered the shares market in the wake of the privatisation programme of the last ten years, and we look at shares and the approaches to investment in them in some detail. The 'fixed-interest' section covers both short-term deposits in banks and building societies as well as longer-term bonds.

The futures and options markets are growing rapidly in size and in the media attention they attract. Don't be 'put' off by 'calls'. The book will explain what they are. However, we believe they are no place for the non-expert investor. But you will be able to hold your own when someone two plates down from you at dinner starts to hold forth on the traded-options market . . .

We do not cover investing in precious metals, or in 'collectibles' like old cars, furniture, fine art or wine. The expertise required to do well in these markets is beyond this book's scope. You should also be aware that we do not deal with foreign investments. Investing overseas can be a good way to reduce the risks involved in investment, but unfortunately it is not possible to do justice to the key considerations in a short book like this.

We focus on UK investments. It's best to start at home with the basics . . .

c h a p t e r · *1*

Some · *basic* · considerations ·

Most investors in Britain today are either too cautious or too gullible. The cautious ones are those who habitually keep large sums of money, for which they have no immediate use, in instant-access accounts in banks or building societies. They are often giving up the chance of better returns from other investments.

The gullible are those who look at the performance of an investment over a recent very short period, and assume that it can safely be projected to continue into the indefinite future. In the late 1980s the supreme examples were those who came to believe that you could never lose money buying a house, whatever the price you paid or the circumstances. The gullible are often encouraged in their illusions by thoughtless journalism.

You do not have to be either too cautious or too gullible. Instead, you can make use of some of the ideas that professional investors use in order that your money can make more money.

Six steps to successful investment ·

There are six main steps for you to master if you want to be a successful investor. This book deals with them in different ways, but they are all important.

Step one:
Know yourself, and your own investment objectives.

This is absolutely critical. Are you concerned about being able to get at your money tomorrow, if necessary? Alternatively, are you willing to put money into an investment and leave it untouched for twenty years? The sensible strategy to follow will look very different in the two cases. There is more about this later in this chapter.

Step two:

Consider all the investment options available.

Until recent years most people in Britain put their money either into property or into 'cash' (bank or building society deposits). Both can be good investments. But this strategy meant that they were ignoring other investments with potentially attractive returns. This book looks at most of the major types of investment available to the small investor in Britain today.

Step three:

Be realistic.

We'd all like to become enormously rich overnight. Unfortunately this is impossible. There is no sure-fire way of getting rich quickly. You should distrust anyone or anything that says otherwise. Normally the scheme being proposed by one of these miracle-workers is fraudulent, extremely risky, or both.

It's always a good idea to remember that the investment world is a highly competitive one, filled with intelligent and enthusiastic people like you. Suppose that just a few of these people discover that something (for example, a share) is sure to be worth £1000 tomorrow. In their scramble to get their hands on the thousand, these keen buyers will push the price up to close to a thousand today.

The returns from investing in completely safe things have not been and are unlikely to be very large. You'll tend to get better returns, on average, for taking risks – a higher level of risk goes with a higher level of return. For example, owning shares usually involves more risk than putting your money in a building society account. The value of shares can fall sharply. But over long periods the average share has offered a much higher return than has the building society. Being realistic about investment means understanding this 'risk-return trade-off'. There's more on these issues in the rest of the book.

Step four:

Diversify.

This means reducing risk, both by having funds in more than one type of investment, and by owning a variety of items of any one investment type where performance can differ widely (particularly shares).

Diversification is about avoiding unnecessary risk by spreading your investments. For example, you can enjoy the higher average returns from shares, and avoid much of the risk involved, by owning shares in several different types of company.

Step five:

Hunt for value.

The prices of different investments go up and down for all kinds of reasons. The successful investor is always looking for investments that are relatively cheap – that is, where the price is well below some measure of the real underlying worth of the item. (The complicated bit is working out what the 'real underlying worth' is, of course!)

It's useful to contrast this approach to investment with a very different one, which is not recommended. One of the factors which drives prices up and down is the enthusiasm of other investors. Sometimes other investors will become very keen on a particular investment (for example, flats in London's Docklands, or shares in an electronics company) and will drive its price up sharply. Some investors try to cash in on such trends: they buy things which may already be 'expensive', but which they think that they will be able to sell on to someone else in a short time for even more. What they are relying on is finding a 'bigger fool' to sell to.

The most successful investors don't try to do this. Instead, they try to buy things which are cheap relative to their underlying value. Investments like these are almost bound to become more valuable eventually, virtually whatever happens.

Step six:

Don't overtrade.

Buying and selling some of the most attractive types of investment (particularly property and shares) is expensive. A sure way not to make money is to 'turn over' your investments frequently, incurring costs each time. You should remember also that many of the people that you deal with when you invest (for example, estate agents and stockbrokers) are paid on the basis of the amount of trading that they handle. They get a percentage each time, and they're not too concerned if your investments do well or not. Their interests are not the same as yours.

Applying the rules ·

This book can help you put some, but not all, of these rules into practice. In particular, the book can't tell you what your investment objectives are, or what your personality is like. Only you can do that. For that reason there is no one absolutely 'right' investment style. What is right for one person is wrong for another.

This book does make certain assumptions, however. It assumes that you're investing to make money, rather than as an enjoyable activity purely for its own sake. It also assumes that, while you are prepared to take a certain amount of risk in pursuit of your gains, you are not particularly keen on risk for its own sake. So it's *not* a manual on how to get rich quick.

Even if these assumptions do 'fit' you, the specific investment strategy you follow should depend on your own personality and objectives. However, it is possible to list a few general points which most investors ought at least to think about:

1 How much cash can you easily get your hands on? If the answer is less than, say, three months' living expenses, give serious thought to building up your cash reserves.

2 Do you own the house you live in? For various reasons it's usually a good investment to own the house that you 'use'. The exceptions are when you don't expect to go on living in the same place for very long, or when house prices are particularly high in relation to incomes (as they were in much of Britain in 1973, 1979 and 1988).

3 Is there a specific purpose for which you will need a set amount of money at a set time in the future? If so, consider investing money in British government bonds ('gilts') which will mature around the time when you will need the money. If you're going to need a set amount of purchasing power, consider index-linked gilts.

4 Having dealt with 1 to 3 above, do you still have money left over to invest? It's often sensible to put at least part of it into shares. Individual shares can be very risky, so buying a 'diversified portfolio' (mixed bag) of shares is a good idea. However, it isn't sensible to split a small sum between many different shares (stockbrokers' minimum charges on buying and selling make it prohibitively expensive). So investors of small amounts in shares should consider diversifying by buying into unit or investment trusts.

*R*ates of return ·

Expected rates of return from different investments are key building blocks in constructing any sound investment strategy. Many people get confused about rates of return. There are a few points to remember:

1   The return from an investment over any period is the profit that you can take out at the end of that period, leaving the amount which you originally invested intact. If your £1000 turns into £1100, that is a return of £100 (or 10% of your original investment).

2   Returns are usually expressed as an annual rate. A return of 10% per year turns £1000 at the start of a year into £1100 at the end. If it takes three years for £1000 to become £1100, the annual rate of return is only 3.2%.

3   Returns are usually quoted in 'nominal' money terms, which take no account of inflation. While this is simple, it can also be highly misleading.

Unless you're a miser, you're not interested in money for its own sake but in what money can buy. So what you care about is not the 'nominal' but the 'real' return on your investments. The real return is the return after allowing for inflation. If your £1000 turns into £1100 in a year but the inflation rate is 7% in that year, the real buying power of your investment at the end of the year is only £1100 ÷ 1.07 = £1028, a real return of 2.8%. This is (almost) equal to the nominal return of 10%, minus the inflation rate of 7% (which is an easier but less accurate way to do the same calculation).

This book is for people who aren't misers, so it mainly talks about real returns. It's often a good idea to try to check out any nominal return that's quoted in 'real terms'.

4   Real returns are typically a lot lower than nominal returns! It's useful to have some idea of what 'typical' real returns are. History is our best guide to this. Because there can be wide variations in returns from year to year, it's sensible to look at long historical periods.

Since the Second World War, the real returns on the main forms of UK investment, before tax, have been:

Shares	6% a year
House Prices	2% a year
Government Bonds	−1% a year
Building Society Accounts (after tax)	−1% a year

A negative real return means that, after inflation, you would actually have lost on your investment. There's more in the chapters on each of the individual investments about why the rates of return have been what they've been, and on the key factors that will determine how they might perform in the future.

5   Small real returns, 'compounded' over a long enough period, add up to large total returns. The beauty of compounding is that you earn 'interest on interest', so that the absolute rate of growth of your investment speeds up over time.

For example, a return of 6% per year turns £1000 into £1060 after one year, but into £3207 after 20 years. By year 20, the £3207 is increasing in value by 6% × £3207 = £192 each year.

Watch out for advertisements where total returns are turned back into annual returns without taking account of compounding, and so give a misleadingly high value. In our example, someone might say that a rise from £1000 to £3207 is a rise of 220.7%, 'so that the annual rate of return was 220.7 ÷ 20 = 11%'. Not so! The investment earned only 6% each year, but the amount that the 6% applied to was getting bigger each year.

The table below shows the power of time and compound interest clearly:

£1000 turns into:

Period (years)	Rate of return, % per year						
	0	1	2	4	6	8	10
1	1000	1010	1020	1040	1060	1080	1100
2	1000	1020	1040	1082	1124	1166	1210
3	1000	1030	1061	1125	1191	1260	1331
5	1000	1051	1104	1217	1338	1469	1611
10	1000	1105	1219	1480	1791	2159	2594
20	1000	1220	1486	2191	3207	4661	6727
30	1000	1348	1811	3243	5743	10 063	17 449
50	1000	1645	2692	7107	18 420	46 902	117 391

The message of the table is: if you want something, start saving now! Patience is a great asset in investment.

6   The returns you get from an investment can be seriously affected by the costs of buying and selling it.

For example, it's quite possible for the costs involved in a small share trans-action to add up to at least 5% of the value of the shares, perhaps wiping out the typical real return over a whole year. The more expensive an investment is to buy or sell, the longer you must hold it to make up for the costs you incur in buying or selling it.

Risk ·

Another aspect to be aware of in setting investment strategy is risk. Risk varies greatly between investments and there are many different ways of measuring it. One good measure is of the variability of returns from a type of investment. Clearly an investment which offers a return of 30% one year but −20% the next is riskier than one which gives you 5% each and every year. The diagram below 'ranks' the historical variability of real inflation-adjusted returns on a one-year basis.

Least risky   ————————————————————▶   Most risky

Building Society . . . Houses . . . Bonds . . . Shares . . . Futures & Options

---

It is important to think clearly about risk, and treat tables like this one with caution. The point is that risk, as far as you're concerned, depends on your objectives. If what you're worried about is having a specific lump sum at a specific date in the future, an investment that delivers precisely that (for example, a government bond maturing on that date) is risk-free as far as you're concerned. However, it's day-to-day performance might be highly erratic, and it could show up as highly risky in a diagram of the sort shown above.

The riskiness of investments depends on the time period being considered. For example, building society accounts are shown as being less risky than houses on a one-year basis. On a ten-year basis, however, houses have historically been slightly less risky – they tend to hold their real value better in inflationary periods. Another point to bear in mind is that, particularly over longer periods, steady but poorly-performing investments can eat into your wealth. Risk always has to be considered together with return.

For these reasons this book looks at risk in various different ways. In particular, it looks at your chances of actually losing money in different types of investment, based on the historical evidence.

*D*iversification ·

'Diversifying' your investments is about spreading them, to reduce the overall risk. 'Don't put all your eggs in one basket' is the oldest and most direct statement of the diversification principle. The main types of investment will often perform differently in a given time period. If shares are doing badly, there is at least a chance that government bonds are doing well, and quite a good chance that house prices are rising rapidly. This means that it's a good idea to have some money in several of the different types of investment if possible, particularly if you dislike risk.

*H*igh rolling ·

As was said above, this book assumes that you're not too keen on taking risks. For that reason, it's not a primer on how to get rich quick. However, it's worth remembering that this is not the only possible approach to making money.

As a contrast, consider the activities of Donald Trump. Trump is a billionaire American property developer (there's more about him in Chapter 2). He has got rich quick and has created a huge fortune by his involvement in a succession of larger and larger commercial property projects. Like other developers, he puts a small amount of his own, and a large amount of other people's, money into projects. As long as the project (after costs) increases in value at a faster rate than the rate of interest on the borrowed money, Trump makes a handsome profit. He sells out, takes his profit, and can reinvest a larger amount in a bigger project. By dealing astutely and adding value in a favourable business climate, Trump has made a fortune.

If borrowing most of the purchase price to buy property sounds familiar, that's no accident. Millions of people in Britain today are doing precisely that. The difference is that most people don't think as big, deal as astutely, or move on as quickly as Trump. While many of them think they would like to be as rich as Trump, they would regard his activities as intolerably risky. After all, suppose it all went wrong and they were left owning a building that was worth less than their mortgage? In that sense they don't 'sincerely want to be rich'.

The point of this is not to criticise a cautious attitude, but just to emphasise that people's attitudes to risk are different. Trump writes that 'I've never gambled in my life'; he also states that 'I don't do it for the money. I've got enough, much more than I'll ever need. I do it to do it. Deals are my art form.'

This book is not designed for budding Donald Trumps. However, even if you are one you should get some benefit from reading it. After all, you have to learn to walk before you can leap!

c h a p t e r · 2

*P*roperty ·

Doris Wills bought her house in Fulham for just £800 in 1948. In 1988, it was valued at £160 000. Even after allowing for inflation the real price had increased by a factor of 15!

In early 1984 a small two-bedroomed flat in Notting Hill Gate, also in West London, could be purchased for under £50 000. In the middle of 1987 the same flat sold for just over £100 000.

Such stunning examples of money for nothing more than sitting at home have led the British to believe that buying a house is the biggest and best investment that they can make. This chapter looks at why this is no longer necessarily the case – and at the factors you should take into consideration before buying.

*P*ropping up the property market·

There are three reasons why most people think property is such a good investment. Two of them have to do with special features of property which don't apply to other investments.

The first attractive thing about property is that you can live in it, unlike, for example, a share certificate. This is very useful if you need somewhere to live, but much less relevant if you've already sorted that out and are looking for somewhere to put your money.

The second thing is that in recent decades buying a house has been, for most people, the only way to borrow money very cheaply. But this cheap money is far less likely to be around in the future.

The final reason is the rapid increase in house prices, which the table below demonstrates:

Year	1956	1968	1978	1983	1988
Average house price (£)	2230	4650	16 300	28 600	56 000
Average price (1988 £)	20 800	30 100	34 900	36 000	56 000

Sources: Building Societies Association; author's estimates

Between 1956 and 1988 average house prices in Britain increased by a factor of about 25. Over the period since 1938 the factor is about 100.

More importantly, the 'real' price of houses – that is, prices with the effects of inflation taken out – went up by a factor of about 2.7 between 1956 and 1988. That's equivalent to an average rate of just over 3% per year – which is a modest return on your investment. However, as the examples above made clear, at some periods and in some places the rate of increase has been considerably faster than that (real increases were particularly large in 1971–3 and 1985–8).

Benefits of ownership ·

An accurate analysis of the attractions of property as an investment must take account of whether or not the popular view of the benefits of home ownership is the correct one.

Let's look at the pros and cons of owning a house in more detail.

Is there no alternative?

At the start of 1988, 64% – almost two-thirds – of the dwellings in Britain were owner-occupied. Most of the rest were council houses, available only to people in the right place and on the right list. Only 8% of dwellings were available for private rental, often not in the right place or the right condition.

As a result, many people in Britain today own property mainly because they have to live somewhere. Owning a house is for them like buying food or owning a stereo. They have no alternative; they are not deliberately choosing property as the place to invest their wealth. We'll call these owners 'house-users', and distinguish them from people who choose to put money into property, whom we'll call 'investors'.

Many people are both house-users and investors at the same time and in the same house, of course. These people own and live in a bigger house than they can really use themselves, or in a house in a more expensive area than they would choose if they were renting. Many of them may not even be fully aware that they are doing this. You should be aware of the distinction, because the financial results can look very different for house-using and investing.

The house-user's hidden income

The rent that house-users save from owning rather than renting can be thought of as a sort of income. After all, if house-users didn't own their own houses they would be paying out rental money from their income to keep a roof over their heads.

Government statisticians assume that the rental value of a house each year is about 3% of its market price. That means that you should be able to rent a house worth £100 000 for £3000 a year, or about £60 a week. In practice, open-market rents are much higher than this. They usually range between about 6% and 8% of market value. Council rents are usually lower than the open-market level, of course.

House-users aren't taxed on these savings in rent, either. This can be a large benefit. You are taxed on income from almost all other investments, such as, for example, the dividends that you get from owning shares. Living in your own property is thus very favoured by the tax system. For example, suppose you own and use a house which it would cost £100 a week to rent. If your tax rate is 25%, this is worth £133 a week to you in before-tax income. If your tax rate is 40%, it is worth £167 a week before tax.

Finally, increases in the value of the first house that you own and live in aren't subject to capital gains tax. This is less important than it sounds. Unless you're very rich, it usually isn't too hard to avoid capital gains tax.

House-user or house-investor?

For the house-user, the amount of money saved by owning rather than renting depends on what they would otherwise have had to rent. However, for 'investors' who own a bigger or more expensive house than they really need this benefit is not available – unless they become landlords and take in rent themselves.

So, if you are not prepared to take in tenants, 'house-using' is much more financially efficient than 'house-investing'. Even if you do take in tenants you are liable to tax on any rental income that you get from them, and you also have to pay any costs of finding tenants. So it's unlikely to be as attractive as 'using' a house yourself.

Costs of ownership

Unlike the benefits, the costs of home ownership affect all owners – house-users and investors – in much the same way. Buildings, unlike share certificates, need to be repainted. But one major cost is disappearing! At the time of writing, you have to pay taxes – rates – on your house. Rates vary widely from house to house and between regions, but on average they account for some 1.5–2% of the market value of the house. Rates, however, are being replaced by the community charge or poll tax. This is a tax on people, entirely unrelated to the value of what they own. As a result, while after-tax incomes on average should be unchanged, the cost of owning a house will go down. This, of course, will make home ownership even more attractive. Some economists have estimated that the abolition of rates will drive house prices up by 20% or more.

However, the other costs of ownership will not vanish. They are water rates, insurance, decoration and – most expensive of all – maintenance of all kinds. These costs can vary greatly from one property to another. The best guess is that, on average, maintaining a house in good condition means spending 3–4% of the total value of the house each year.

Profit and loss

So what's the bottom line? Should you be a renter, a user or an investor?

Even after costs of upkeep, house-users are normally much better off than they would be if they were renting (unless they pay a very low rent to a council or private landlord). House-users save up to 6–8% of the value of their house each year by not paying rent, but have to meet costs of 3–4% of the value of the house if it is kept in good repair. Their net gain from owning and using it is highly variable, but may average about 3% of the value of their house each year. Investors (who don't take tenants) lose about the same amount each year: they have the costs, but aren't saving any rent.

These percentage gains and losses don't alter very much from year to year. They may not sound huge. However, as we saw in Chapter 1 small regular annual gains or losses have large impacts on investment returns over a long period. So it's vital for you to be clear in your own mind as to why you're buying a particular house.

Don't let property lead you up the garden path ·

The other main elements which determine how well property does as an investment in the long term are the cost of borrowing, and movements in house prices. These are the reasons people often use to defend their decisions to spend a lot on housing. However, you should be very careful if you intend to buy a house for these reasons – they may actually result in you losing money.

The joy of debt ·

Most people who borrowed money to buy their houses over the last 30 years have, after allowing for inflation and tax relief, actually been paid money by their lenders. This bizarre state of affairs is what has made investment in a house such an irresistible proposition. It has pushed houses through the roof – and persuaded more and more institutions to lend money to house buyers.

But beware; the good times have ended.

What happened was that the rate of interest, after allowing for tax relief, at which borrowers were repaying their mortgages was outstripped by the rate of inflation. After inflation, mortgage money was available at less than a zero interest rate, or at a 'negative real' interest rate in economists' jargon. The point to grasp is that the mortgage rates which most borrowers were paying were well below the rate of inflation in the general economy, let alone the inflation that was occurring in house prices. In effect, the lenders were subsidising the borrowers.

How investors made a killing in Acacia Avenue

Here is a concrete example of how 'lenders subsidising borrowers' worked in practice:

Suppose you buy a house with £50 000 of your own money. House prices rise by 3% in real terms each year for the next 25 years. At the end of that 25 years the house is worth £104 700 in real terms. You have made a profit of £54 700: roughly doubling your money.

Now suppose that instead of putting up the whole £50 000 yourself, you put up only 10% of it: £5000. You get a 25-year mortgage for the other £45 000. Suppose also that for some reason the mortgage lender charges no interest and asks only that you pay back the original value of the loan. This is equivalent, in real terms, to what was happening in mortgage lending for a prolonged period.

After 25 years, your stake in the house would have gone up from £5000 to £59 700 (£104 700 total value of house, minus the £45 000 owed to the mortgage lender). Your profit is £54 700 as in the previous example. However, because your orginal investment was so much smaller, the size of your stake has increased by a factor of 12; that is £59 700 ÷ £5000. That translates into a real rate of return on your money of 10.4% per annum. That's an extremely good investment by any standards.

When to borrow on property

As long as the mortgage rate that you pay (after allowing for tax relief) is less than the rate of increase of house prices (less an allowance for necessary repairs, insurance, etc.), it is profitable to borrow as large a share of the cost of a house as you possibly can. These are the circumstances in which you should be as big a 'house-investor' as possible.

On average, over the last 30 years, the mortgage rate before allowing for tax relief has been about 2% per annum in real terms (i.e. 2% greater than the general inflation rate). But *after* allowing for tax relief at the basic rate of income tax, the effective real cost of borrowing averaged *minus* 1.5% per annum.

The gains from rises in house prices have been very unevenly distributed. Those buying houses with mortgages have done extremely well – the more highly borrowed, the better. Mortgage lenders have done much less well. That means, of course, that people who lent their money to the building societies have also done much less well (there's more about this in chapter 3).

Cheap mortgages

You will now be wondering where you can get one of these very cheap mortgages. Surely heavy borrowing is a guaranteed way to success? The answer is that it would be, if very cheap mortgages still existed.

Since 1980 mortgage rates in real terms have been much higher than they were over the preceding 20 years. At time of writing, the real return demanded by mortgage lenders is of the order of 6% per annum. That means it's now very difficult to make money hand over fist by borrowing to buy property.

One reason for what's happened is that those who lend to building societies have become more and more dissatisfied with the return they've got on their money. To attract the necessary amount of money to fund mortgage lending, building societies have been forced to offer higher and higher interest rates. It requires a very rapid rate of house price increase to justify paying 6% in real terms for a home loan.

The lesson for the future is: watch developments in real mortgage rates carefully, but don't be surprised if the very cheap rates of the past never return.

House prices: the concrete facts ·

We have seen that house prices increased by a factor of 25 between 1956 and 1988. The best estimate is that they rose by a factor of 100 between 1938 and 1988. These huge rises mainly reflect the scale of general price inflation in Britain. But even real house prices (i.e. prices adjusted for inflation) rose by a factor of 2.7 between 1956 and 1988. While this average increase has been bigger than the return from some other types of investment, it's been noticeably smaller than the total return from shares.

The message, even from this period of booming house prices, is clear: unless real mortgage-lending rates are very low, be very careful before you buy a house as an investment. You may well do better in other investments, particularly shares.

A modern myth

Medieval thinkers believed that the earth was flat. Many people in Britain in the late 1980s believe that house prices never fall.

Neither view is right.

Average house prices in Britain fell in five out of the 41 years between 1947 and 1988. The risk of decline is even more marked if you look at real house prices (house prices adjusted for inflation). Real prices fell in 15 years out of 41. While some of these real price declines were from inflated levels reached just after the Second World War, others have occurred in recent years. In 1981, for example, house prices rose by less than 1%. Because the general inflation rate was almost 12%, real house prices fell by 9%. Not a very good inflation hedge!

You should also know that there were 'sustained' declines in average house prices both between 1973 and 1977 (when real prices fell by a total of 36%) and also between 1979 and 1982 (−15%).

It is true to say that, in modern times, real house prices haven't been as unstable as the returns from shares or bonds. If the period since 1956 is a guide to the future, the odds are against real house prices actually falling over any five-year period (only about one chance in six). In this sense, the average house is not a very high-risk investment. In addition, to repeat the obvious, real prices have increased on average: by 3.3% per year in real terms since 1956, or 2.3% per year over the long period since 1947. So believing the myth hasn't done most people too much harm – just as thinking the earth is flat doesn't matter if you're just going down the road.

Remember, however, that you can't buy the 'average British house'. You buy a specific house in a specific place, and that carries rather more risk, as we'll see.

Why house prices rise

Why have house prices risen in this way? With many other goods we expect real prices to fall over time, as people get better at building them. For example, the real price of cars is now much lower than it was half a century ago. Why don't house prices behave in the same way? To get an answer, we have to turn to the economists' favourite tools – supply and demand.

Let's look at supply first. The supply of housing in most of the places in which people want to live is actually very limited. Suppose that the demand for houses doubles in a particular area – London, for example. Is there a rapid expansion of the number of flats and houses in London as a result? The answer is obviously no. Most of the land on which houses can be built in London has already been built on. The same is true of many other areas in this densely-populated island. Shortage of land isn't just a British phenomenon; we can see the same in places like Manhattan and Hong Kong.

Even where land is available it may not be available for house building. This has put pressure on prices in Southern England in recent years. Houses have gone up in price much more rapidly than has the cost of the bricks, building workers, and other items needed to build new homes. Sensing there is money to be made, building firms have tried to get planning permission to build new towns in previously undeveloped areas of Southern England. In practice, they've found it very difficult to get the necessary permission.

No one wants a new town in their own backyard – particularly if they moved to the area they now live in precisely because it was quiet and undeveloped. It's not surprising, therefore, that in the ten years to the start of 1988 the total stock of dwellings in Britain grew by less than 1% per year. The result is still higher house prices.

Demand

Let's look at the increase in the demand for housing. A number of factors have combined to push the demand up sharply. At the top of the list is the rising level of real incomes for most people: as people get richer they seek to buy more and better housing. When this force meets a fixed supply of housing, the result is higher real prices. This point should be stressed. As the chart overleaf shows, there is a close connection between the rate of growth in total real incomes and the rate of growth in real house prices.

make money make money

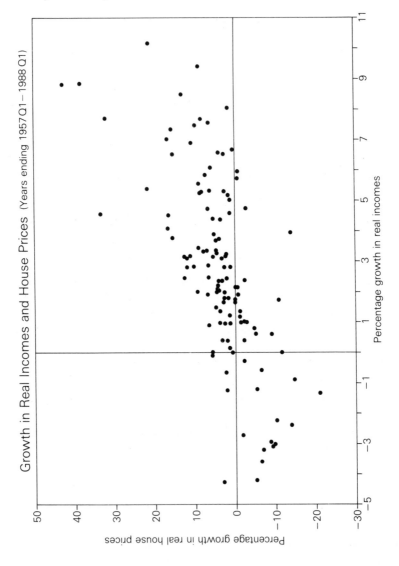

Growth in Real Incomes and House Prices (Years ending 1957 Q1 – 1988 Q1)

Percentage growth in real incomes

Percentage growth in real house prices

Each point on the chart shows a separate 'year' (the period between the first quarter of 1987 and the first quarter of 1988 is one such 'year', and the period between the second quarters of 1987 and 1988 is another 'year', although it overlaps the first). The distance from the left-hand side of the chart measures the rate of growth of total real incomes (after adjusting for inflation and tax) in Britain in that 'year'. The distance up from the bottom measures the rate of growth of real house prices in that year. There is a close association between fast growth in real incomes and fast growth in real house prices.

In the long run, incomes and house prices grow at about the same rate. In fact the chart shows that in the short run the link seems to be something like two-for-one: when real incomes are growing 1% per year faster than usual, real house prices grow about 2% per year faster than usual; when real incomes are growing 1% per year more slowly than usual, house prices grow 2% per year more slowly than usual.

For these reasons it has generally proved most profitable to buy property just before real incomes start to grow fast. This is typically when the economy is relatively depressed but about to recover – for example, 1971 or 1982. Watch the national or local rate of growth in real incomes for clues as to how the property market may behave.

An Englishman's home is his tax shelter

We've already seen that housing is a good thing to be in on, for sound tax reasons. This, too, has helped to push up demand. The tax advantages are:

1   When you borrow to buy a house, the interest you pay on (currently) the first £30 000 that you borrow can be subtracted from your income before your tax bill is worked out. For most people, £30 000 has been and remains a very big proportion of the amount they have to borrow. At a mortgage rate of 12% per year and an income tax rate of 25%, tax relief is worth £900 per year.

2   When you live in your own house, there is no tax on the rent that you save by doing so.

3   When you sell your house, there is no capital gains tax on the profit you have made.

Borrowers who were lucky enough to be repaying a mortgage over the last thirty years were favoured by the fact that their real cost of borrowing was negative, partly because of tax relief (see above).

The herd instinct I: Buyers

The final factors behind higher demand and in the rise in house prices are of a more temporary nature. The first is speculative fever. As more and more people have seen the advantages of housing as an investment, they have tried to get a 'foot on the ladder'. As sometimes happens with shares, price increases attract more 'punters', who push prices up still further. Those who act on this basis run serious risks though.

The herd instinct II: Lenders

The other factor that has been at work in recent years has been increased competition between building societies and other financial institutions, especially banks.

The traditional main sources of mortgage money for house buyers were building societies. In the early 1980s banks could bid more fiercely than before for deposits, and were disillusioned with some of their traditional areas of lending. They saw mortgage lending as a potentially profitable and low-risk area of business, and pushed hard to get into it.

In 1987 only just over half of mortgage lending was by building societies. Other institutions – particularly banks – had captured the rest for themselves. This competition made it easier for house buyers to get home loans. Lenders were prepared to offer borrowers more and more money (relative to borrowers' annual incomes) on easier terms. And, at the time of writing, no one has yet been disappointed. House prices have risen rapidly, and the lenders' money has been more or less secure.

The great property crash?

How high can house prices go? Can they rise, as some people seem to believe, without limit? The answer is no – or at any rate not unless the prices of other things, and average incomes, are rising without limit as well.

While there are examples of 'speculative manias' for things driving their prices up out of all connection with other prices and incomes, this has always been followed by a crash. One salutary example of this was the Dutch speculative mania for buying tulip bulbs in the seventeenth century – culminating in a tulip bulb being given in payment for an entire brewery! Needless to say it all ended with a collapse, and serious problems for the Dutch economy.

House prices and the ultimate deterrent

It's no surprise that the long-term link between the level of average incomes and the level of average house prices is very close. As you can see from the chart overleaf, the ratio of the average house price to average male earnings has fluctuated in a narrow range, normally between three and four, for the last thirty years. In 1988 the average house price was about £56 000 and average male earnings were about £12 700, so the ratio was about 56 ÷ 12.7 = 4.4.

This is the ultimate control on house prices. The economic booms of 1971–3, 1978–9 and 1983–8 pushed up real incomes fast, and real house prices faster. The house price-to-earnings ratio rose each time (to almost five in 1973). But this was unsustainable. In fact, when average house prices are more than four times average earnings, houses are likely to prove a poor investment relative to other things.

Someone who has a mortgage four times their annual income at an interest rate of 12% per year is paying out 48% of their income in interest alone, never mind capital repayments. Anyone in such a situation is likely to be vulnerable. A period of reduced income (due, say, to unemployment, or just less overtime) or of high interest rates will ravage their finances. If there are many people in the same position house prices will stagnate while incomes and mortgage costs are brought back into balance.

Predicting house prices ·

The long-term increase in house prices is likely to continue to be closely linked to the long-term increase in incomes. Real incomes (adjusted for inflation) have traditionally increased by 2% or 3% each year. There's no reason to expect that to change very much, so we can expect that real house prices will do the same. This is not fantastic, but not at all bad.

There are special factors at work in the late 1980s, though. The abolition of the poll tax lowers the cost of house ownership for a given price, so that will push up prices.

make money make money

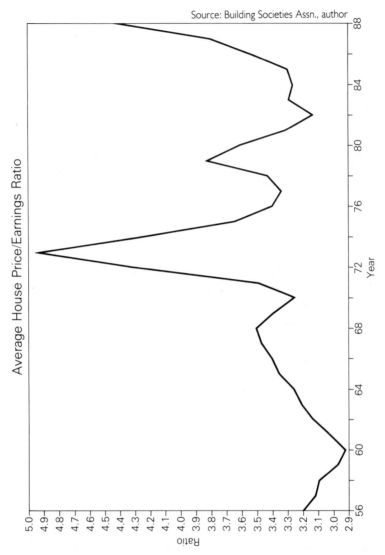

Source: Building Societies Assn., author

Average House Price/Earnings Ratio

Year

Ratio

However, the factors working in the other direction are more important. At the time of writing (late 1988) the house price/income ratio is historically very high. This suggests house prices will at least stagnate until incomes have risen again. Also, mortgage interest rates have recently increased sharply. House prices will certainly fall relative to incomes, probably fall relative to other prices, and possibly fall in money terms. All the indicators are what you would expect them to be before a slump in property prices.

Safe as houses?

The other side of the equation is the lending side. The house price boom has been based on lenders being prepared to lend high, and sometimes increasing, multiples of income to first-time buyers. This will only stop if the lenders find there is a significant number of people unable to repay the loans. But as yet the rate of failure to pay mortgage interest has been extremely low. Indeed, the default rate is lower than that for any other form of borrowing. However, a worrying sign is that the rate has been rising – still to very low levels – in recent years.

Could it all go sour?

If the banks, building societies and other financial institutions involved in mortgage lending ever became convinced that mortgage lending was not 'as safe as houses', then the whole happy process could go into reverse. Lenders would start lending lower multiples of borrowers' incomes, and demanding more security – perhaps much higher deposits – from borrowers. Their managers would also want them to set aside a higher proportion of their borrowed funds against the risk that mortgages would not be repaid. These factors would push up the price of mortgage money, in turn damping down demand. Again this would act to depress house prices.

A vicious cycle of default, weakening lender confidence, weakening borrower confidence and falling house prices could develop. This would be in sharp contrast to the virtuous circle that we've seen develop in the UK in the past ten years. However, it would be similar to the experience of the United States during the 1930s.

Aberdeen

You may think this is far-fetched. However, there are recent regional examples of the same thing happening on a small scale. In the UK the most striking example is that of Aberdeen.

In the late 1970s and early 1980s the Aberdeen property market boomed. The reason was that local employment and incomes were expanding rapidly due to the prosperity of the North Sea oil industry. In early 1986 the world price of oil fell sharply. At the new lower price it no longer made sense to explore for high-cost oil in the North Sea. Hard-pressed oil companies cut their exploration efforts. This had a dramatic effect on the Aberdeen job market. It also had dramatic effects on the property market.

House prices stopped rising, stabilised, and started falling. Many people wished to leave Aberdeen. Potential buyers had no jobs to come to. To sell their houses sellers were forced to take lower prices than those ruling just a few months earlier. Indeed, there were many cases of people simply abandoning their houses. Once the market value had fallen below the value of the mortgage outstanding, it no longer made sense to go on paying the mortgage. At this point the building societies were forced to take possession of defaulting borrowers' houses – the last thing they intended, and certainly the last thing they wanted.

Texas – fading Lone Star State

A similar situation has occurred – again as a result of the oil price collapse in the mid-1980s – in Texas. There, there had been much speculative building on the back of oil-led prosperity. Because it takes time to build new properties many were still being built when the oil price collapsed. Once they were finished they added further to the glut on the market. The result was, and at time of writing still is, massive vacancy rates for both residential and commercial property in Texas; and falling property prices.

Texas has given a new building term to the English language – 'see throughs'. These are skyscrapers which you can literally 'see through' because no one has rented space in them. There is a rich crop in the Texas state capital, Austin.

Prices and geography

The experience of Aberdeen and of Texas points up a serious problem with property investment. You are likely to buy property near where you work.

If you work in an industry which is a major employer in the region you live in, then the fortunes of your work and of your property investment are likely to be tied closely together. If your industry does well, you and your area will probably become more prosperous, and the value of your property investment will do well also.

However, the downside risk is considerable. If the main industry in your region does badly, for whatever reason, there will be lower incomes around to support property values. In the worst case, as some of those in Aberdeen found, you might find yourself out of a job and with property which was rapidly falling in value. So property investment is riskier in areas with a single dominant industry.

It's less risky in an area with a diversified employment base – for example, London and the south-east of England. Having a single dominant industry increases the chances of both boom and bust. The worrying factor is that if the 'bust' happens, it may strike at your job as well as at the value of your property.

Money tied up in property ·

Another problem with property investment is that it is very hard to get at your money in a short period of time. This is known as market illiquidity. One ICI share is identical to another, so it's easy to find buyers when you have to raise money, although you'll have to take the going price. A house is much more specific. It takes time to 'match' your house with a buyer who is ready to pay what you regard as the going price.

In addition, the whole process of selling or buying property is a very expensive one – involving hiring estate agents, payment of stamp duty, or the cost of advertisements that you place yourself. The emotional strain involved also seems to be higher than in dealing in other types of investment. For these reasons, rapid buying and selling of property is good for neither your bank balance nor your health. Property investment is not for anyone who needs to be able to get at their money in short order.

Do these problems completely overturn the popular idea that property invest-ment is a good thing? The answer is: not really, if you are a 'house-user'. The long-term record is, and continues to promise to be, reasonable. If house prices go on rising in line with average incomes, rather than in line with other prices, they are likely to increase at about 2-3% per year in real terms. In addi-tion, a 'house-user' enjoys a saving in rent which is likely to be well in excess of the costs of maintenance. When these two sources of 'return' are combined, they add up to a good return for the relatively low risk involved.

Getting a profit from the chosen land

It's important to be realistic about how you can get at your profits from property. The only real access that most people have to the profits from owning their own property is when they 'trade down'. That means either moving to a smaller house or to a cheaper area. Both of these choices are realistic ones for people in the later stages of their lives, when their children leave home or when they retire. At that point property investment in a booming area can leave one with a healthy nest-egg; until then, however, it may be difficult to get at the wealth that you've built up in property.

Borrowing to invest in property ·

Borrowing heavily to invest in a house is now only worthwhile if you are sure that the property will rise rapidly in price. Clearly this means looking carefully at factors like the property's proximity to jobs. This may sometimes still be a viable investment strategy; at the time of writing, however, in most parts of the country the ratio of house prices to average incomes is at or close to an all-time high. That makes this kind of investment very risky.

The ratio of house prices to income could go still higher, of course. But the odds are against it. The long-run control on house prices is income levels. So the likely outcome, in the parts of the country where house prices have risen sharply, is that prices will fall relative to incomes. If you're borrowing at high real interest rates to finance such an investment, it probably won't be very profitable.

A second home

What about buying a second home? Again, this may be for house-use pur-poses. You may really want the country cottage because you've always wanted to live in the country at weekends. The 'return' you get from doing so may then be adequate on its own: the investment aspects are secondary.

But if you're doing it mainly as an investment, the advice to you would have to be: don't. There are two reasons. First, the tax advantages evaporate. If you keep it empty, there is no tax relief on the borrowing you need to purchase the second house. On the other hand, if you let it out you're liable to income tax on any rent you receive. Either way, you'll be liable to capital gains tax when you finally sell a second house. It can also be very difficult to get a reliable rental income from tenants. You need to find the tenants in the first place; this probably means paying agents' fees, which can be considerable.

The other problem is the risk that your rental income may be artificially held down by rent controls. At the time of writing, rent controls on new private tenancies are being reduced, although controls remain in place on most existing tenancies. This may mean that politicians are learning that 'rent control seems in many cases to be the most efficient technique so far known for destroying cities' (Assar Lindbeck, *The Political Economy of the New Left*, Harper and Row, 1971).

*I*nvesting in residential property ·

There are five key points to remember:

1   Investment in a house is different from using a house. An investor isn't saving rent. He has nothing to offset against costs, unless he becomes a landlord.

2   House prices in the long run are closely tied to incomes. Real incomes grow at about 2–3% per year in the long run, and so do real house prices. When prices are high relative to incomes it isn't usually a good time to buy. Remember the general investment principles identified in Chapter 1: 'be realistic' and 'hunt for value'.

3   A key to doing well is choosing the right location: that is, one where property prices are low in relation to the prospective level of incomes in the area. Watch for general business developments in an area, and also for transport developments which may make an area easier for more buyers to get at – or, alternatively, bypass. Again, hunt for value.

4   House prices can fall, particularly allowing for inflation. This can happen either because the ratio of prices to incomes has got too high just because prices have raced ahead, or because local incomes have collapsed. If you can, 'diversify' – don't put all your money into property.

5   It can take time, and cost a lot, to get at money invested in property. So in terms of our general principles, 'know yourself' (when will you need the money?) and 'don't over-trade'!

*T*he Big Time ·

There may have been more fortunes made, faster, in property development than in any other industry. This may make it appealing to you. However, those fortunes were not made by simple investment – by buying shares in large property companies, for example. When shares are freely traded in the market their price tends to be close to a 'fair' one; you can usually hope for a return in line with that from other shares, but for no more than that. (Shares are covered in Chapters 4 and 5.)

Successful property developers don't just put 'passive' money into a project and sit back and wait for the returns to roll in. Instead they are at the centre of what can be an extremely complicated business. It's rather like being the conductor of an orchestra – find a site, find a new use for it and a potential new user, find builders, find money, get round government controls, and put the whole lot together at minimal cost. If you can do all this, good luck . . .

Trump: The art of the deal

Donald Trump is a billionaire. He did not inherit his money. He is still relatively young (he was born in 1946). He has invented nothing tangible. He is able to devote a considerable part of his time to charitable work. Yet he is one of the most-discussed business heroes of America in the late 1980s. He owes it all to property investment.

Trump has taken the principles described above to their logical conclusion. He has developed a succession of commercial and residential property complexes in the North-eastern United States (especially New York), using each as the stepping stone to the next bigger one. Each location has been carefully chosen – with fundamental attractions, yet not yet fully 'discovered' by business for one reason or another. He has used a mixture of borrowed private and public money for most of the financing, and been quick to sell long leases on completed properties to new users.

Trump puts the deal together, collects his percentage, and moves on. It's a form of organising genius. Do it often enough and you can become very rich very fast. You can go broke too. So far that hasn't happened to Trump – he's been skilful, and lucky. Luckily for us, he has written down how he does it in his own book, *Trump: The Art of the Deal* (Century Hutchinson Ltd, 1988). He lists eleven key principles which he tries to follow. They are all listed below, along with an attempted interpretation of the less obvious ones.

1   Think big.

2   Protect the downside and the upside will take care of itself. By this he means minimise risk whenever you can; as was suggested in Chapter 1, Trump's ideas on what is an acceptable level of risk are different from most other people's.

3   Maximise your options. If no one wants a new office on your site, perhaps you could use it for flats.

4   Know your market.

5   Use your leverage. Find out what other potential parties to your deal want or need, and be in a position to give or deny it to them.

6   Enhance your location. Don't just develop a site in a good area, per-suade people that where you have your site *is* the good area.

7   Get the word out. There is no such thing as bad publicity.

8   Fight back. Against critics or bureaucrats who try to get in the way.

9   Deliver the goods.

10   Contain the costs.

11   Have fun.

While the specific mixture of these ideas which Trump puts to work is designed for the highly-charged world of large-scale New York property development, it's interesting to note how many of them are applicable anywhere.

A point that Trump does not mention, although it is central to his rapid accu-mulation of wealth, is the role of borrowed money. An estimate in late 1988 put Trump's borrowings at 55% of the value of his property. This is a classic strategy, of course; but as we saw earlier in the chapter, it may be much less applicable in Britain now than it has been in either post-war Britain or Donald Trump's America.

c h a p t e r · 3

Cash · and · bonds: fixed-income investments ·

This chapter is about what are called 'fixed-income investments'. They are those investments where it's guaranteed that you'll get a set amount of money back at some time in the future (often the amount you first put in). Normally, you'll also get a specified rate of interest in the intervening period. Fixed-income investments include the different types of bank account, building society account and National Savings account, as well as bonds issued by governments and companies.

It may seem strange to include a chapter about fixed income in a book called *Make Money Make Money*. The popular image of these investments is that they don't offer much in the way of profitable opportunities. I believe that this view is misplaced, in its way as much of a myth as the notion that house prices always go up. There are times and circumstances when fixed-income investments are very attractive. The purpose of this chapter is to try to give you some idea of how they can fit into a successful investment strategy.

The thing that is different about fixed-income investments is that they can be completely safe. If you're prepared to hold on to the asset for a specified period of time, you're guaranteed to get your money back (at least).

Sleeping on it

Of course, you could guarantee that you get your money back simply by keeping it under the bed. To get you to lend it to them, the people who want to borrow your money have usually got to offer rather more than that. What they will offer is a fixed rate of interest for a specified period. The rate of interest is always above zero, because otherwise you'd be better off keeping the money under the bed.

Making a percentage

For example, a building society may offer to pay an interest rate of 5% per year on an account. That means that if you put £100 into an account now, you get £105 back in a year's time. The additional £5 is what's needed to get you to lend the money to them.

The important thing is that you're guaranteed that your money will be returned to you. That's different from investment in property, in shares, or in the more exotic assets like futures or options. With those investments there are no guarantees of any sort. As a result, they're not for the faint-hearted. Nor are they for those who want to get at their money at a specified time. The natural place for these people to put their money is in the fixed-income market.

Getting fixed

However, not all fixed-income investments are alike. They differ in a number of ways. The most important distinction is between those investments where you're guaranteed to get your original investment back at any time, and those where this is not certain. In the first camp are deposits with banks, with building societies, and some investments in National Savings; in the second are investments in bonds.

Bonds are longer-term fixed-interest investments where eventual repayment of a set amount is guaranteed, but this can be many years away. In the meantime, if you want your money back you will have to sell the bonds in the open market – just like shares or property investments. The ruling price in the open market may be well below, or well above, the price you originally paid for the bonds – again like shares or property. It may also differ considerably from the price that you will eventually get for the bonds if you hold them to maturity.

Capital-certain investments ·

Some assets keep your investment (capital) completely secure. Bank deposits and building society accounts are the major competitors for money in this market. The differences between banks and building societies are getting harder and harder to spot. The institutions, and the investments they offer you, are growing more alike.

It's worth looking at the sheer scale of our investments in these institutions. At the end of 1987, sterling bank deposits averaged some £1400 per man, woman and child in Britain. Building society deposits were even bigger – around £2400 per head. National Savings deposits of various sorts totalled about £700 per head. When multiplied by the total population of the country, we're obviously talking about huge assets. It's quite clear that many people want the security that fixed-income investment gives them.

Banks ·

The 'fixed-income institutions' haven't always been as similar as they are today. Banks, for instance, grew up providing money transmission services to business people. They were – and still are – open for only part of the business day, and not at any other time.

A better class of mattress

They offered, above all, security. Your money was safe in a bank current account. In addition, you could write a cheque on that money. As a result you could use it as if you had the cash in your hand – at least if whoever was selling something to you would accept a cheque! As far as the banks were concerned, the fact that they offered security and this money transmission service was quite sufficient.

In effect, bank current accounts offered – and still offer – a superior version of keeping your money under the bed. They didn't have to offer you interest as well. You got a (low) rate of interest if you could put your money in a deposit account, which didn't provide instant access to the money. Only under massive competitive pressure from the building societies have banks felt compelled to start offering interest on current accounts.

Building societies ·

The building societies grew up in a very different way. They were originally co-operative societies where members banded together to save small amounts of money, and to use the total saved to finance the building of their own houses. At first they were small-scale affairs; as they grew nationally, more and more people became members of them.

There were three main reasons for growth. First, for many people building societies were the only route through which they might get access to the finance needed to buy a house. It's hard to remember now but the banks used not to trouble themselves much with this kind of lending. As home ownership became a realistic option for more and more people, they naturally turned to the building societies to provide that finance. Building societies, in turn, naturally gave priority to those who'd already saved with them. This was particularly important when mortgage money was very scarce. Instead of rationing it by price (that is, charging a high interest rate so that borrowers only wanted what was available), the societies decided who got mortgage money by length of membership. Mortgage money was cheap, but the people who got it were those whose grandparents had had the foresight to open accounts for them when they were very young.

The second reason why people turned to building societies for fixed income investment was that they usually offered a higher return. This was possible because the societies didn't have to bear the costs of the money transmission service, and because they were more motivated to reward savers. The third reason was a practical one. Building societies were open at more convenient times than banks: the branches of societies usually stayed – and still stay – open until late in the afternoon on weekdays, and opened on Saturdays.

The pressure of this competition, and a gradual relaxation of restrictions on building societies, has produced a convergence between the two sets of institutions: banks and building societies are becoming more and more alike. Competition has proved a very powerful force for change.

Ready access versus higher returns ·

Some things don't change, however. As before, there is still a trade-off in the investments offered by each institution. Both banks and building societies generally offer a trade-off between access to funds and the rate of return that's available from them. The longer that you're prepared to leave your money with the bank or building society, the higher the rate of interest you'll get. If, on the other hand, you need to be guaranteed instant access, you pay for this through getting a lower rate of return.

The logic behind this is simple. If a bank or building society has to call in money at short notice, borrowers will be less keen to borrow from it. As a result, long-term loans usually command higher interest rates. This in turn means that if you are prepared to invest for a longer period of time, you can get some of the benefit of this higher interest rate.

By putting your money in a short-term deposit, you are giving yourself the option of taking it out with no, or very short, notice. You may never use this option, but having the option is going to cost you money. For this reason, it's important to think about the likely pattern of your financial needs. If you're prepared to give up instant access to your money, then you can have a higher interest rate.

Both banks and building societies also offer you a higher interest rate if you deposit more with them. For example, by putting more than £5000 into an account with some societies you'll get an extra 1% per annum in interest payments. This can be well worth having.

Again the logic here is simple. From the bank or building society's point of view there is as much work to be done in processing a £5 investment as a £5000 one: their costs are the same whatever the size of your account. As a result, if you invest more with them they can spread those costs over a bigger asset base; some of those savings can be passed on to you. So it's not worth having a large number of separate accounts with different institutions. You'll normally be better off concentrating your holdings in one or two institutions and benefiting from a higher interest rate.

Because banks and building societies are increasingly competitive in the products they offer, neither this book nor any other can give you a guide that will be good for all time as to where you should put your short-term money. The options available are always changing. The best thing to do is to stay well informed – by looking at the financial pages of daily and Sunday newspapers, for example. The *Financial Times* carries a comparative table called 'Interest Rates: What You Should Get For Your Money' every Saturday. Remember, what you're looking for is a combination of the access that you need to your money and the best rate of interest available.

Tax facts

One important factor to bear in mind is your tax position. Interest on bank and building society deposits is normally paid after deduction of 'composite rate' tax. What this means is that, if you pay income tax at the basic rate (25 pence in the pound at the time of writing), you need pay no more tax on this interest. If you pay income tax at a higher rate, you have to pay the difference.

Some investments – notably some National Savings deposits – pay interest tax free. That makes them particularly attractive to those who are higher tax-rate payers. Other investments offer a higher pre-tax return and so are more suitable for those who pay no tax.

Many advertisements about short-term investments quote returns on more than one tax basis. For example, a bank deposit may pay X% per year after deduction of composite-rate tax, which is 'equivalent to a gross return of Y% per year' (this means that a basic-rate taxpayer would have to get a pre-tax interest rate of Y% to do as well). All this can get confusing. The critical thing is always to compare after-tax rates of return, at your rate of tax, between different investments. You care about the returns you get, not about what the tax man gets.

No hiding place ·

No investment can completely escape the gyrations of the economy. Money under the bed loses its spending power as prices rise. Putting money into building society or bank accounts is a good or bad move according to how other investments are performing relative to the interest rates which fixed-income accounts are paying. The thing that determines what fixed-income investments will pay out is short-term interest rates.

The going rate

Short-term interest rates fluctuate. They are set by the government, although the government's freedom of action in this area is seriously restricted by wider economic developments. But once the government sets a rate all other rates tend to fall into line around it. This happens because of competition amongst borrowers for money: if banks raised the interest they paid on deposit accounts and building societies didn't, many investors would switch to banks and the societies would find themselves starved of funds. So when banks' base rates go up, building society deposit rates – and the other side of the coin, mortgage rates – follow fairly promptly.

That doesn't mean that all short-term interest rates are the same, by any means. Some are markedly higher than others, depending on the institution you invest with and on the rules controlling your access to your money. However, rates do all tend to move up and down together.

Watch out – inflation's about ·

In this section, we look at the historical returns from a typical building society share account, net of basic-rate income tax, as a good example of what an ordinary investor has been able to get on short-term fixed-interest investments. As noted above, building society deposits have tended to pay higher interest than bank deposits.

The table below shows the returns over different periods since the Second World War. The data comes from Barclays de Zoete Wedd's *Equity-Gilt Study*. (BZW is a firm of stockbrokers: more use is made of their historical data elsewhere in this book.) All the figures are for the calendar years shown, including those at either end – so '1946–87' runs from January 1946 to December 1987. The returns assume that each year's interest, net of basic-rate income tax, was reinvested.

Period	Average return % per year Nominal	Real
1946–87	4.9	−1.4
1968–87	6.7	−2.8
1978–87	7.5	−0.4
1983–87	6.5	1.9

As usual, the important returns are the real (inflation-adjusted) ones, which appear in the right-hand column. You're concerned about what is happening to the real purchasing power of your money. On average, returns from short-term fixed income since 1945 have not been enough to offset inflation. The real inflation-adjusted return of −1.4% per year can be put another way saying that if you had put £1000 into such an account at the end of 1945, by the end of 1987 its buying power would have fallen to only £550. Once you correct for changes in prices, fixed interest hasn't been a good bet.

Risk

In fact, putting money into a building society share account has also been 'risky' in the sense that in just over half (23 out of 42) of the years since the

Second World War, you would have lost money in real terms. This is a worse record on the face of it than that for investment in shares, which is usually thought to be a lot more risky. However, this poor 'risk' record of short-term investments is a bit misleading. Most of the losses in 'down' years have been relatively small. In only one year (1975) was the real return from a building society account worse than −10%. In shares, on the other hand, there were several years of large losses (more about those in Chapter 4).

1980s gains · · ·

In recent years, however, real returns on building society share accounts have been positive. Indeed, they were positive in each of the years 1982 to 1987 inclusive. If you had put £1000 into an account at the end of 1981, it would have had a real purchasing power of £1130 by the end of 1987. Why is this the case? From the table it's clear that nominal interest rates have remained at the historically high levels of the 1970s, while the inflation rate has been much lower.

· · · follow 1970s losses

It's useful to look at the factors behind these high rates, so you can judge if they are likely to continue. Why have nominal interest rates stayed high? There are three factors at work.

1   Investors suffered very badly in the 1970s when high inflation eroded the value of their savings. Indeed, the years of positive real interest rates from 1982 followed 12 years in succession (1970–81 inclusive) of negative real rates. £1000 put into the building society at the end of 1969 was worth £2260 by the end of 1981, but this would have had a buying power of only £510. Investors are now rightly suspicious of low nominal rates of interest; they demand compensation against the risk that inflation will rise again.

2   The government has sought to keep interest rates relatively high. This, paradoxically, has been part of the government's battle against inflation: the idea is that if it costs us more to borrow, and we get more from saving, you and I are less keen to spend and this helps to hold prices down.

3   A final factor has been the high level of real interest rates around the world. We cannot wholly insulate ourselves from global trends: real interest

rates have been high in most countries, a reflection of lower savings rates and high government borrowing – particularly in the United States.

Short-term fixed-income investment is a better deal at some times than at others. It's a particularly good deal when inflation is low but has recently been high, and when the government is holding interest rates up to keep spending down. This description fits the late 1980s in Britain very well. I believe that the odds are that the factors which have made for better-than-usual returns in recent years will continue. But it's important to be realistic about the returns that you can expect from investments which, as we noted above, are only really a better class of bed to hide your money under. Even in 1983–7 returns (after tax) were only about 2% per annum in real terms.

What will happen if inflation rises again? We have seen that in the past short-term fixed-income investments have proved to be only a partial defence against high rates of inflation. Although investors are more wary about inflation now, it's still likely that a resurgence would lead to poorer real rates of return from fixed-income investments.

Summing up

This asset class will never be a way of getting rich quick. In present circumstances it is at least a way of maintaining the value of your assets, and perhaps getting a bit richer more slowly. What it does offer is great safety and ready access to your money. So it makes sense to use short-term fixed-interest investments as follows:

1   To provide cash reserves for emergencies – perhaps equal to three or six months' living expenses.

2   When you know you will need a sum of money for a particular purpose (wedding reception, new car, etc.) in the near future.

3   When you think other types of investment are particularly risky so that you want to play safe.

*B*ond is beautiful ·

Beyond the security of the bank and building society lie a whole family of fixed-income assets which are more dependent on fluctuations in the national and world economy for their current value. One fascination of these investments, which can be lumped together as 'bonds', is that it is possible to explain exactly how both their capital value, and the rate of return they offer, change with external fluctuations. Studying them is rather like being able to gaze into the mechanism of a Swiss timepiece. This is not possible with shares or real estate, where there are no precise equations which hold income and capital value together.

As it is possible to do this with bonds, this book goes to some trouble to lay their mechanism bare. If the investor understands how they work, bonds are one of the most useful instruments that he or she can utilise.

*B*onds ·

Bonds are long-term fixed-interest debt. They are issued by companies and governments – particularly governments. What happens is that the government takes the investor's money now and promises to repay it in, for example, 20 years' time.

To get the investor to part with his or her money, the government pays a fixed rate of interest. This is known as the 'coupon' on the bond. For example, a bond may carry a 10% coupon: that means that for every £100 the investor will get back when the bond matures (perhaps in 20 years' time), he or she will get £10 every year until the maturity date.

Why do governments issue bonds?

One good reason is that people don't like paying taxes. However, they do like the benefits that the government provides for them through public expenditure. Public expenditure pays for motorways, social security, defence, and the many other things for which the government has assumed responsibility.

The government can pay for public spending in three ways. It can raise taxes – which is rather unpopular. It can print the money – but this tends to lead to higher inflation. Thirdly, a rather attractive way of raising the money is simply to borrow it. That means that today's voters will get the benefits, but tomorrow's (or next decade's) will pay back the money.

There's a less cynical reason for borrowing. Many of the projects that the government undertakes will provide benefits over a long period of time – a new road, for example. It's only sensible to match these long-lived public assets with long-term public liabilities. Just as the road will yield its benefits over (say) 20 years, so the voters can pay for it over 20 years.

Man is everywhere in bonds

There's nothing mysterious about bonds. Indeed, they are a very important type of asset ('asset class' in financial parlance). At the end of 1987 the UK government had issued bonds with a total market value of £137 billion. That's about £2500 for every man, woman and child in the country. Corporate bonds accounted for another £10 billion at the end of 1987.

Gilts

This chapter focuses on the UK government bond market, because it's so much larger and because government bonds carry no credit risk. The government won't default on its bonds because it can always print the money it owes. Private companies are not in this happy situation, although it should be stressed that the bonds of 'blue-chip' (large and secure) UK companies are also very safe. Because they've always been regarded as being extremely safe, UK government bonds are often called 'gilt-edged' securities, or simply 'gilts'. They're as safe as gold.

However, it's important to notice that, unlike bank or building society deposits, bonds are only completely safe if you're willing to hold them to maturity. This can often be a long time in the future. You may have to wait for 20 years or more before you're guaranteed to get your money back. At the time of writing, there is one gilt which will not mature before the year 2024.

If you need to get at your money you can always sell in the active 'secondary market' in gilts. In the secondary market gilts are traded amongst holders in much the same way as shares. As is the case with shares, prices fluctuate. If you need to get at your money in a hurry you'll have to take whatever the going price is.

Bond prices

What determines the going price of a bond? Let's suppose that the market rate of interest is 10% per year, and that it's expected to remain 10% per year for ever. If the government issues a 20-year bond with a 10% annual coupon, it can sell the bond for £100 now for every £100 it promises to repay in 20 years' time.

For as long as the present and expected rate of interest stays at 10%, £100 will remain the going price of the bond in the market place. Comparing the coupon of £10 per year with the price of £100 shows that the 'interest yield' or 'running yield' on the bond is 10% per year. As there will be no change in price between now and the day the bond matures in 20 years' time (no capital gain or loss), the interest yield of 10% is also the total rate of return ('redemption yield') on the bond if it is held until it matures.

Suppose you buy this bond for £100. Suddenly, and to everyone's surprise, the market rate of interest decreases to 8%. What is your bond worth now? Remember, it promises to pay you £10 a year every year for the next 20 years, and then to pay £100 back at the end. The question really is: what would a new purchaser be willing to pay for this set of guaranteed future cash receipts now? £10 per annum is 8% of £125. So, if there was going to be no capital gain or loss on the bond, the new buyer would be prepared to pay £125. Then his investment would yield 8% each year, in line with the market rate of interest.

However, we know that the bond will be redeemed (bought back by the government) for £100 in 20 years' time. So, if the new buyer did pay £125 he would take a capital loss. That detracts from the total return – the redemption yield is lower than the income yield.

In practice the price of your bond will rise to a bit less than £125: to £119.79 to be precise. At the new price, the income yield is higher than 8% per year (£10 ÷ £119.79 = 8.35%, in fact). It's higher by just enough to offset the capital loss that a new buyer will suffer when the bond is eventually redeemed for a mere £100 as opposed to the £119.79 he paid for it. The key point is that the price of the bond today adjusts so that the *total* return (redemption yield) that a new buyer gets is exactly 8% per year.

You can either choose to sell your bond for a profit of £19.79, or to hang on to it. Remember, if you reinvest the money you may only be able to get 8% on it somewhere else.

To sum up so far · · ·

1   The price of bonds fluctuates with the market rate of interest.

2   When interest rates rise, bond prices fall. When interest rates fall – as in our example – bond prices rise. The longer-lived is the bond, the more its price moves up and down.

3   The maturity of a bond is the length of its life; which ends with 'redemption' when the investor usually receives the amount it was originally sold for.

4   The coupon of a bond is the number of pounds paid in interest, for every £100 of redemption value, every year of its life.

5   The interest yield on a bond is the coupon as a percentage of its current market price.

6   The redemption yield on a bond is the overall percentage return the investor will receive if he or she holds the bond until it is redeemed. This figure takes into account both coupon income and gains or losses in capital value.

Interest rates

If interest rates set the price of bonds, what sets interest rates? As we saw above, the short-term rate of interest is determined by government policy. The government, through the Bank of England, moves short-term interest rates up and down depending on how it wants to influence the national economy. When the government wants to stimulate the economy, it will go for low interest rates. If, on the other hand, it is trying to restrain a booming economy it will raise interest rates.

We also saw above that because one short-term fixed-income investment is a fairly good substitute for any other short-term fixed-income investment, the rate that the government sets will be transmitted throughout the market. So, when the rate which the government sets is relatively low, so too are bank base rates, building society deposit rates, mortgage rates and the like.

Why long-term gilts usually give better interest rates than Building Societies

What matters for long-term bonds is what short-term interest rates are expected to do over the whole life of the bond. The alternative to buying a 20-year gilt is just to put the money in a building society account or something similar and leave it there for 20 years. That way, your money will always be earning whatever the short-term rate of interest happens to be. Sometimes it will be high, sometimes low.

So to attract you to buy long-term gilts, the total rate of return (redemption yield) will have at least to match the average short-term rate that you expect from the building society. In fact, because the price of the gilt will fluctuate during its life, whereas you're always certain to get your money back from the building society if you need it, you'll probably need a higher expected return from the gilt before you buy it. Redemption yields on long-term gilts will only be below today's short-term rate if the short-term rate is expected to fall in the future.

The Gilt Market – as seen in the *FT* ·

Now let's look at the money-making opportunities in the gilts market in more detail. The total value of all the gilts outstanding is well over £100 billion. All the individual issues are listed in the financial pages of newspapers – normally at the top of the shares section. In the *Financial Times* they are listed under 'British Funds', in ascending order of maturity.

There are about 100 different issues. They range in maturity from very short-dated bonds – maturing perhaps in a couple of months' time – to those which will probably never be redeemed. The *FT* breaks them up into 'shorts' (up to five years before maturity), 'five to fifteen years', 'over fifteen years' and 'undated'. There is also a group called 'index-linked', which are inflation-proof bonds; there's more about them on page 64. Each issue is identified by its name, coupon, and redemption date. The names don't mean anything – there's no practical difference between 'Treasury', 'Exchequer' or 'Funding'. It's the coupons and the redemption dates that do matter.

Redemption dates

The redemption date or maturity that you go for will depend on whether you think that the overall trend of interest rates will be higher or lower than the market expects.

There are two points to watch about redemption dates. The first is that, for some gilts, they're quoted as a range: for example, Treasury 12% 2013–2017. That means the government can choose when to redeem the bonds, between the dates mentioned. If the market rate of interest is above the coupon, so that the bond is selling for less than £100, the government will leave redemption to the last possible date. It won't pay £100 for something worth less than £100 until it has to!

'Undated' bonds have no definite redemption date, they also have very low coupons and are selling at well below £100 and so are unlikely ever to be redeemed. All the return on these gilts is coupon income. If you buy them now you're buying a flow of coupons that will run for ever, but the only way you can get your original lump sum back is by selling the gilts on to someone else: in the meantime, the price may have moved against you . . .

Coupons – as seen in the *FT*

Recall that the coupon is the amount which a gilt will pay out, as a proportion of its redemption value, each year. There is a big range of coupons on offer. They range from 2½% to as much as 15½%. Why is there this range? Part of the answer is simply tradition. Governments have normally tried to sell new gilts at around £100 per unit, when the final redemption value will also be £100. That means that there will be no capital gain or loss to the first buyers of the gilt. All the return, therefore, has to come from the coupon. So the 2½%-coupon bonds were issued at a time when investors expected roughly that total return from a bond. Similarly with the 15½%-coupon bonds.

Can you make most money in gilts by just buying issues with high coupons? Sadly no. Like the shares market, the fact that there are many expert investors in gilts means that there aren't obvious easy profits to be made.

Redemption Yields and Interest Yields – as seen in the *FT*

The gilts section of the *Financial Times* shows both the interest yield and the redemption yield. A look at it will show that bonds of similar maturities but different coupons usually have similar redemption yields. (The exception is bonds with very low coupons, which are discussed below.) The market adjusts the prices of gilts with different coupons so that their redemption yields are roughly the same. What happens is that the market pushes up the price of bonds with high coupons, thus lowering their income yield and increasing the capital loss that will be suffered by a new buyer.

Consider once again our example where all redemption yields are 10% per year. A 20-year bond with a 15% coupon will sell for £142.90. A one-year bond with a 15% coupon will sell for £104.65. In any case where the coupon is above the redemption yield, a gilt will sell for more than par (£100). This means that the interest yield (coupon divided by price) will be lower than the coupon, and that the redemption yield (interest yield, minus effect of capital loss) will be lower still.

*P*laying the Bond Market ·

The whole pattern of bond prices, and the redemption yields (also known as 'yields to maturity') that go with them, is driven by investors' expectations about what will happen to short-term interest rates in the future. So the critical decision to make in bond investment is: has the market guessed future interest rates right? If it hasn't, then you can make big profits, or suffer big losses, by holding bonds. These capital gains or losses happen on top of the interest yield that you'll get from the bond whatever happens. Remember that it's not enough just to get the trend of short-term rates right, if the market's got it right too. If both you and other investors expect short-term rates to fall, and they do, the price of bonds won't change. Bond prices already had the fall in short rates built into them.

Let's suppose that you think that interest rates are going to fall but the market doesn't believe that. Let's say the market expects short-term rates to stay at 10% for ever; however, you expect that rates will fall soon to 8% and stay there for ever. How should you play the market? We saw in the example earlier that, if you're right, the price of a 20-year gilt with a coupon of 10% will rise from £100 to £119.79 if the redemption yield falls from 10% to 8%. How does this compare with, for example, a one-year gilt with the same coupon? In fact the price of the one-year gilt will rise only from £100 to £101.89, a profit of less than one-tenth of that on the 20-year gilt.

Volatility

This is a general principle: the price of bonds with a long life ahead of them ('long-dated' bonds, or sometimes just 'longs') is much more volatile than that of shorter-dated ones. In the first chapter we saw that a fixed gap in the rate of return between two different investments each year adds up over longer and longer periods to bigger and bigger differences in their value. Bonds have the same feature: there is a fixed repayment when the bond eventually matures; the further away that date is, the more impact the rate of interest has on what that future repayment is worth today.

Beating other investors

The result is that longer-term bonds offer bigger opportunities for both gain and loss than shorter-dated ones. If you believe that interest rates are going to fall and stay down, you should buy longer-dated bonds (as long as other investors don't expect an even bigger fall). If, on the other hand, you think that interest rates are going to rise, you'd be better off in shorter-dated bonds. They carry less capital risk, but also less opportunity for capital gain. Indeed, if you're very confident that interest rates will rise, you'd want to be out of bonds entirely and have your money in something like a building society account, where the capital value of your investment is not at risk.

Tax

In fact, you may well be better off buying gilts with low coupons than with high coupons. The reason is tax. One of the advantages enjoyed by investors in gilts, because the UK government wants to encourage this form of investment, is that capital gains on such investments are tax-free.

Coupon income, however, is subject to income tax, but there are ways to minimise its effect on your total return from gilts.

Suppose that you are paying income tax at a rate of 40%. Suppose also that you are investing in 20-year gilts, all of which have redemption yields before tax of 10% per year. If you buy a 20-year gilt with a 10% coupon it will cost £100. Two-fifths of each year's coupon will be taken away at your 40% tax rate, and the effective after-tax return on the bond will be only 6% per year. But a 20-year gilt with a 3% coupon and the same redemption yield of 10% will cost only £39.94. Because a lot of the return in this case comes from non-taxable capital gain (the rise in price to £100 at maturity), the after-tax return is 7.76% per year. If the redemption yields are the same, a taxpayer will find it better to buy the low-coupon gilt.

In fact, a look at the redemption yields shown in the *Financial Times* reveals that the redemption yields on gilts with very low coupons are a bit lower than those on other gilts. In other words, because taxpayers are keen buyers of low-coupon gilts their price has been forced up. However, it usually isn't forced up very far; it's normally still a good idea to choose low-coupon gilts if you pay income tax (particularly if you pay at more than the basic rate), but to choose high-coupon gilts if you don't pay tax.

To get some idea of your after-tax return from a gilt you can do the following calculation:

1   Take the interest yield today. In our example of the 20-year gilt with the 3% coupon, this is £3 ÷ £39.94 = 7.51%. For any real gilt this value is published in the *Financial Times*; it's the taxable income of the gilt today. (Remember, the total return or redemption yield – 10% in our example – includes capital gain.)

2   When it is nearly mature the price of any gilt will be close to £100, so the interest yield at the end of its life will be very close to its coupon. To get an idea of the average interest yield over the whole life of the gilt, add the current interest yield to the coupon and divide by 2. In our example this gives 7.51% + 3% = 10.51%. Then 10.51% ÷ 2 = 5.26%. By averaging the interest yield today and the interest yield when the bond matures we get an idea of the 'lifetime' taxable income from it.

3   Multiply this number by your current income tax rate. This stage gives an idea of the income tax payable on this gilt at an annual rate. In our example of the 40% tax rate, 5.26 × 40% = 2.10%. If you have any way of predicting your future tax rate, use that number instead.

4   To get a rough measure of the after-tax return per year, subtract the income tax payable from the before-tax redemption yield. As we've seen, the redemption yield is available from the *Financial Times*. In our case this gives a result of 10 − 2.1 = 7.9%.

As you can see, it's very close to the true value of 7.76% which was worked out using a computer (quoted in the 'Tax' section opposite). You can treat any other gilt in the same way.

Tax is taxing

As in the case of short-term fixed-income investment, or indeed any other investment, your concern is always with what you get from your money after tax. There is no simple way of measuring the exact return you'll get from a gilt after tax, even if you're an avid reader of the financial pages. The maths is just too complicated! In any case, you need to make an assumption about the rate of income tax you'll be paying throughout the life of the gilt. That's likely to change, either because your circumstances change, or because the government alters tax rates.

Returns ·

This section looks at the returns that you can expect from investment in bonds. For most of this century these returns have been disappointing.

Victorian values

In the nineteenth century when there was effectively no – or very slow – inflation, yields on long-term gilts averaged about 3% per year. Indeed the 'high noon' of Victorian civilisation as far as bondowners were concerned was the year 1896, when bond prices got so high that the yield on long-term gilts fell to the lowest level ever recorded, 2.2% per year.

I don't believe that we'll see rates that low again in the foreseeable future. Neither does the gilts market. We'll look into the reasons in more detail later on. The point to note here is that Victorian investors seemed happy to accept a real rate of interest of about 3 or 4% per year. There was no allowance for inflation built into bond yields, because there was no inflation. Prices were regulated by the gold standard. It would not have occurred to an investor in the last part of the nineteenth century that sustained inflation, of the sort that we've seen in this century, would be possible.

The 3 or 4% per year real return that Victorian investors got from gilts has not been achieved in the twentieth century. If one of your ancestors had invested in gilts at the end of 1918, the total real return to the end of 1987 would have averaged only 1.1% per year. Indeed, over long periods of this century, the real return from gilts has been negative. For example, had you invested in gilts at the end of 1945, your real return to the end of 1987 would have averaged −1.2% per year. Over 42 years, £1000 would have shrunk to just under £600 of equivalent purchasing power. As we'll see in Chapter 4, the same investment in shares would have grown to £12 500 in the same period.

Since 1945, the return from gilts has been very little better than the after-tax return from a building society share account. That doesn't make sense in terms of risk and return. We know that short-term investment is less risky than long-term fixed-income investment, yet the former did almost as well.

The year-to-year real returns from gilts have been highly risky. We'll see in Chapter 4 that, for shares, seven out of 42 (one in six) post-war years involved real losses of 10% or more; for gilts, the figure is ten years out of 42 (almost one in four). (The source of all the statistical information in this section is the Barclays de Zoete Wedd *Equity-Gilt Study*; the numbers assume that your ancestor bought a portfolio of long-dated gilts, that no tax was paid, and that all coupons were reinvested.)

Inflation the enemy

The villain of the piece is inflation. We have seen in the section on short-term fixed-income investments that interest rates tend to move at least in part to reflect inflation. When inflation rises, higher interest rates mean lower bond prices, and so capital losses, for people who already own bonds. It also has to be remembered that rising inflation reduces the real value of the payments that you get from holding bonds. Therefore, inflation is a particularly vicious enemy for investors in bonds.

In fact, the real problem is unexpected inflation. If inflation is rolling along smoothly, investors can anticipate it. If you're sensible you'll only buy bonds if they offer a big enough return to compensate you for the inflation that you expect. But by definition you can't foresee unexpected inflation! So it isn't built into bond yields. The problem for bond investors after 1945 was that the era of usually stable prices before the Second World War led people to think that this was the normal state of affairs. They were gradually disillusioned.

There isn't a wholly reliable measure of unexpected inflation, but one simple measure is to look at the inflation rate compared with the rate in the previous year. (The idea is that people have got used to last year's inflation rate; if this year's is different, that's probably a surprise.) In the table below we split the 42 individual years between 1946 and 1987 into those when the inflation rate rose and those when it fell.

	Years	Average percent change	Years when real return on gilts was: Positive	Years when real return on gilts was: Negative	% of years positive	Average return from gilts
Inflation Rising	17	+3.9	5	12	29	−6.8
Inflation Falling	25	−2.6	15	10	60	+4.1

The results are clear-cut. Gilts are a much better investment when inflation is falling.

Index-linked gilts ·

Rapid rates of inflation in the 1960s and 1970s have had several major effects on the bond market. One of the most important has been that the government decided, in 1981, to introduce what are essentially 'inflation-proof' gilts: they are known as index-linked gilts because the government promises to increase both the coupons, and the final redemption amount, in line with the Retail Price Index.

Suppose that an index-linked gilt is launched alongside an ordinary one. Both have 20-year lives. The ordinary gilt pays a coupon of, say, £10 each year and is finally redeemed for £100. However, there is no sure way of knowing what you will be able to buy with either the coupons or the redemption amount, because there is no sure way of knowing what will happen to prices in general over the next 20 years.

With the index-linked gilt, the coupon and the redemption amount rise in line with prices. Suppose that the first year's coupon is set at £2 (index-linked gilts have low coupons). If prices in general are 50% higher after five years, the coupon will have been moved up to £3. If prices in general are six times higher after 20 years, the final coupon will be £12 and the gilt will be redeemed for £600. Whatever happens to inflation, investors are protected.

You can track index-linked gilts in the same part of the financial pages as conventional gilts – for example, under 'British Funds' in the *Financial Times*. As with conventional gilts, the coupon and redemption date are part of the name of each gilt ('Treasury 2% IL 2006'). Redemption yields on index-linked gilts are shown in real terms, so they are much lower than the redemption yields of ordinary gilts. (In fact two real redemption yields are shown for each issue – the reason is that, for administrative reasons, the precise real yield on an index-linked gilt does still depend very slightly on the inflation rate.)

At the time of writing, the redemption yield on the longest-dated conventional gilts is just under 9% per year. The real redemption yield on the equivalent index-linked gilt is 3.5% per year. But this is 3.5% per year in real terms. Index-linked gilts carry no inflation risk.

It's hard to resist the conclusion that index-linked gilts can offer a very good investment opportunity. At the yields just quoted, they offer a return at least as good as that achieved by conventional gilts in the golden age before 1896; far better than that from conventional gilts in recent times; and not too much lower than the long-term return from shares, at far less risk.

You can obtain a form to buy these index-linked gilts at large post offices (more about this below).

Won't get fooled again . . .

The gap between the real redemption yield on index-linked gilts and the standard redemption yield on conventional gilts is a measure of the extra return investors need as compensation for the inflation which they expect, and for taking the chance that inflation will actually turn out to be even worse. At the time of writing, this gap is about 5½% per year. Numbers like these get out of date quickly, though. You might like to get a newspaper and check today's numbers yourself.

However, it is worth noting that 5½% is slightly more than the average inflation rate of the mid- to late-1980s. This means that at present investors are suspicious that inflation will be higher in the long run. Certainly they do not believe that the government will succeed in its stated aim of getting the inflation rate down to zero.

Quite clearly, another reaction to high inflation in the 1960s and 1970s has been great mistrust about future inflation rates on the part of bond-market investors. Despite inflation rates below 5% per year for most of the mid- and late-1980s, yields on conventional (not index-linked) long-dated gilts rarely went much below 10%. Investors have been 'burnt' too often. They now demand extra protection for holding conventional bonds.

Home owners versus bond owners

This caution is appropriate. One of the results of the spread of home ownership – discussed in Chapter 2 – is that many more people have a stake in at least mild inflation. Remember, we saw that house prices more than kept pace with inflation. Indeed, in this century they have proved to be the most reliable medium-term hedge against inflation of any of the main investment types.

On the other hand, most property owners have bought their properties with mortgages which are fixed in money terms. They are betting – at least implicitly – that inflation will help them out with the real burden of their debts. They expect that a mortgage which is burdensome now, i.e. takes a large proportion of their income, will soon be eroded by inflation.

Any government which seeks to reduce inflation from its rather low levels in the mid- to late-1980s (around 5% per annum) to smaller numbers or to zero faces a huge political obstacle. Few people really have an interest in stopping inflation now. There are far more votes in the hands of first-time owner-occupiers than there are in those of wealthy holders of conventional bonds. The bond investors are not stupid, however; they have decided that they need a substantial yield 'cushion' against the days when inflation may reaccelerate.

Know your gilt

Should you invest in conventional gilts? As is the case with other types of investment, neither this book nor any other can make your mind up for you. Circumstances in the market change rapidly, and so specific advice quickly gets out of date. The other point to remember is that even at any one time a gilts strategy which suits one person may not be sensible for another.

You should be aware of the pitfalls involved. Gilts have performed poorly in recent decades, although the tide turned in the 1980s. The key problem has been inflation, and particularly unexpected inflation. If you're optimistic that inflation will stay under, or be brought under, control, then gilts are for you. My own view is that inflation is under imperfect control. As a result, I would say: tread very carefully. Because of the risk that inflation poses for conventional gilts, they should certainly not be the only asset that an investor looks at.

Other influences which you should be aware of include the rate at which gilts are being sold into the market by the government, and world interest rate/ inflation trends. At the time of writing the government is running a large budget surplus, so it is a net buyer of gilts – which tends to support their prices.

A practical exercise

One exercise you can go through if you're thinking about investing in gilts is to compare their redemption yields with the latest inflation rate. Find out the redemption yield on a gilt with about, say, 20 years to maturity. Then subtract the latest inflation rate – this is the percentage increase in the Retail Price Index over the past year, which is frequently reported in the press. What's left is a very crude measure of the real yield on conventional gilts.

Since 1945 this value has usually been greater than zero (about three-quarters of the time); it has also been unusual for it to go much above 4% – that's happened only about one-fifth of the time, much of it in the 1980s, as described above. So you can easily see if gilt yields are high (attractive) or low compared with recent inflation.

This is only a crude measure because what you're interested in is future inflation, not past inflation. However, there's often a fair amount of 'inertia' in inflation, so one year's value can be a guide to the next. To get a fuller picture, you could also try to check other indicators which are a guide to future inflation:

1   What's happening to pay (average earnings)? Because labour is a major part of the cost of production, rises in pay usually get passed on. A very rough rule of thumb is that, if average earnings are rising by X% a year, prices will tend to rise by about X – 3% per year.

2   What's happening to oil and raw material prices in sterling terms? These are other, though less important, parts of production costs. Remember that, even if world prices of oil and raw materials are subdued, their sterling prices can still rise if the pound falls against other currencies; and a falling pound also pushes up the price of imported finished goods.

In an ideal situation, redemption yields on gilts should be much higher than the current inflation rate, and the other indicators should suggest that inflation was going to stay low or fall further. Then you could invest enthusiastically in gilts, with a good chance of getting capital gains (from falling yields, and so rising capital values) as well as good coupon interest. Strangely, this ideal situation hardly ever comes about . . .

There is no sure-fire way of knowing when to get involved in the gilts market. Remember that, as elsewhere, many other investors are competing with you. They too are assessing what's happening to inflation and the other influences on the market, and driving prices up and down accordingly. However, going through an exercise like the one above can help to focus your own thinking on what's likely to happen.

Other bonds ·

So far, this chapter has concentrated on gilt-edged bonds. There are several reasons for this: they are almost completely safe, in that there is no doubt you'll get your money back (although, as we've seen, what the money will buy is another matter); they are much the largest part of the market; they offer a wide choice of coupon and maturity, and also the index-linked option.

Although you can invest in other bonds too, it usually won't be sensible for you to do so. One reason is given above: other bonds are almost always less safe than gilts, and can be much less safe. This is a particular problem for the small investor. While an institutional investor can buy many different lower-quality bonds, on the basis that the higher average yield will pay for the odd disaster, small investors can't spread themselves that far. The other reason is that it's usually much more expensive for a private investor to deal in bonds other than gilts. However, it's worth knowing a bit about bonds other than gilts, if only to know where to be wary.

Eurobonds

The most rapidly growing part of the non-gilt market in recent years has been the Euro-sterling market. This is part of the glamorous Eurobond market.

The first thing to realise about the Eurobond market is that it is not particularly European. What is distinctive about it is that it is subject to no national regulation. It started in the mid-1960s: Americans were spending a great number of dollars abroad, in payment for various goods and services; many of these dollars ended up in the hands of people who had no wish to convert them back into their own domestic currencies. The dollar was a safe and attractive currency; companies saw this pile of homeless dollars as a borrowing opportunity.

What was needed was a way for companies who wanted to borrow in dollars to get those dollars from investors who had them. They could already do this through the domestic US bond market, but regulations there were relatively onerous. It was also difficult for foreign investors to get involved: in the first place, America was far away; secondly, the coupons from investment in bonds in the American domestic market were subject to 'withholding tax' – coupons were paid after being taxed at source.

The invention of the Eurobond got round both of these problems. European banks brought out ('lead-managed') dollar bonds on behalf of well-known companies. The bonds were part of no existing market, nor subject to any regulations; they paid coupons which were often untraceable by the investors' local tax authorities.

The Eurobond market had and has no nationality. That is precisely its attraction. The market grew and grew. The major players invented the rules around it as they went along. Although it started with Eurodollars, it rapidly developed into a market where bonds in many other currencies could be bought and sold. Thus there are Euro-yen bonds, Euro-guilder bonds, Euro-sterling bonds, and so on.

Because this book is not about investing in foreign currencies, we'll look only at the Euro-sterling portion of the market. That's already relatively big. At the end of 1987 the total nominal value of Euro-sterling bonds outstanding was about £25 billion. Remember, these bonds are covered by the same rules as other Eurobonds – there are no rules. The bonds are in 'bearer' form: once you've bought them, to claim your coupons or have them redeemed you simply have to turn up at the right place with the right piece of paper. No questions will be asked either about where the money with which you bought the bonds came from, or when and how you intend to pay tax on your coupon income. (It should be pointed out at this stage that failing to declare taxable income to the Inland Revenue is an extremely serious offence.)

You don't have to venture into Euro-sterling to find bonds that aren't gilts. There are also bonds issued by companies and by non-UK borrowers in the UK domestic bond market (known as 'bulldogs'!). These are subject to UK regulations. The non-gilt markets offer a huge range of issuers, coupons and maturities. However, most issues tend to be smaller in size than is usual in the gilts market, and spreads between buying and selling prices are usually wider. So it's more expensive to deal in bonds that aren't gilts.

Risk businesses

Bonds rank higher in the pecking order than shares when a company gets into trouble. In theory, at least, bond-holders always get their money paid back before shareholders see a penny. Less melodramatically, companies pay out interest to their bond-holders as one of the costs they deal with before profits are worked out. The investment effect of this is that, while coupons on bonds are fixed, they usually get paid; whereas although dividends on shares can grow, they tend to fluctuate. That's the main reason why shares are a riskier investment than bonds – and why, on average, they have to offer a higher return to the investor.

But there are degrees and degrees of safety in bonds. Investment in the bonds of a reputable government, or a blue chip company, is almost completely safe – you are pretty certain to get your money back. (I have to point out once again that, unless you hold a bond until it matures, the price you get for it is uncertain; and that if you do hold it until it matures, the money that you get back may not be worth as much as the money you put in in the first place.)

Junk bonds

Some issuers, however, are much less secure. Where an issuer's credit quality is shaky, the bonds that it offers must yield a higher return to attract investors. When an issuer is thought to be very insecure, the bonds are known as high-yield or 'junk' bonds. These can offer mouth-watering returns, but the reason for this is that you may not get all, or indeed any, of your money back. The borrower may not be in a position to pay you interest, nor redeem your bond, in a few years' time.

Many companies in the US have issued junk bonds, particularly those involved in ambitious takeover battles. The junk bond division of US investment firm Drexel Burnham Lambert, led by Michael Milken, orchestrated both enthusiastic issuing and buying of high-yield bonds in the 1980s. As yet, few sterling bonds fall into the high-yield category – although Drexel Burnham Lambert are seeking to expand their UK business. However, some bonds do yield much more than others. For example, at the time of writing you could buy bonds issued by Pemex, the Mexican state oil company, which have a redemption yield of about 5 per cent per year more than that on a comparable gilt.

As with most other investments, the investor in high-yield bonds is making a choice about risk and return. You don't get something for nothing. Most investors would prefer gilts to Pemex bonds if the yields were equal, believing that there is a greater risk that Pemex won't be able to pay them back. As a result, the yield on Pemex bonds is higher by just enough to persuade investors to hold them.

The investors who go into such bonds are consciously taking a risk. You should leave this kind of risk-taking to the professionals; private investors are not usually well equipped to distinguish good junk from bad. You will do better to limit your decisions to those on the position you have in low-risk bonds (gilts). Another advantage is that you can deal more cheaply in gilts than in other bonds.

*B*uying and selling gilts ·

Stockbrokers can and do buy and sell bonds for private clients. However, for the small-scale private investor a better way of buying gilts is through the Post Office. The 'National Savings Stock Register' (NSSR) operates a scheme which allows investors to buy and sell a wide variety of all the gilts which have been issued; you can get the list at your Post Office. Collect the relevant form, fill it in, and send it with a cheque to the scheme's head office in Blackpool. Orders are processed as soon as possible – although obviously a few days after you've decided to deal.

The major attraction of trading in gilts in this way is that the commission is fixed at a relatively low 0.4% of the transaction's value (with a minimum of £1). This means that an investment of £1000 in gilts will cost you only £4 in commission.

Stockbrokers, on the other hand, typically set the same charges for gilts as they do for buying and selling shares. This almost always involves a higher commission rate, with a considerably higher minimum charge. The advantages in going through a stockbroker are that you can deal in gilts which are not on the NSSR list, and that you can deal straight away rather than rely on the post. However, one gilt behaves in much the same way as another of similar maturity and coupon; and day-to-day price movements in gilts usually aren't very large. So I don't think that these factors come close to off-setting the cost savings of going through the Post Office. For all except very large investments, this is much the most attractive way to play the gilt-edged market. It's surprising that more people don't know about this route. Certainly stockbrokers don't publicise it . . .

Using either route, your gilts will be bought in the open market from a 'market-maker'.

One of the results of the 'Big Bang' financial industry reforms of 1986 was that far too many firms became market-makers in gilts. At the time of writing there are still far too many; as a result they compete frantically for business. The spreads between bid and offer (the prices at which the market-makers will buy or sell) for gilts are very narrow – about 0.1 or 0.2% of the price, much smaller than for most shares.

Managed funds ·

Another route into bond investment, in either gilt-edged bonds or Euro-bonds, is through managed bond funds. They work in the same way as unit trusts, which are discussed in Chapter 5. As with unit trusts, you are entrusting your money to the guidance of professional managers. That carries risks all of its own. The best way to minimise those risks is to invest only in reputable firms, with records which they are pleased to show you and which have been audited by an independent authority.

In fact, the advantages of hiring professional managers in the gilts market are limited. Gilts all come from the same stable, and can be easily compared in terms of only one or two characteristics (maturity, coupon, redemption yield). So there isn't much benefit from in-depth professional research. Gilts of similar maturity and coupon behave in similar ways. So you don't need to hold many separate issues in order to reduce risks. Unlike shares, the benefits of diversification are fairly limited. Finally, dealing costs can be low – there isn't much lost by buying in small lots.

Summing up on bonds ·

Investment in bonds may be for you if you want something a bit more exciting than short-term fixed-income investment but less risky than investment in shares. The major source of bonds, particularly for small investors, is the government. With the bonds of a reputable issuer, like the government, you're sure of getting regular coupon payments and your investment redeemed when the bond matures. However, the value of bonds fluctuates during their life, so they're not risk-free unless you can hold them to maturity; and they're never risk-free in real terms, because you don't know what a given amount of cash at maturity will buy.

In a well-ordered world the returns from bond investment would reflect its risk level – returns would be higher than those from building society deposits, but lower than those from shares. That's proved only partially true in the past. For most of the period since 1945 bonds have done rather poorly in the face of faster-than-expected inflation.

Bond is back?

Will bonds do better in future? The key point to remember here is that bonds represent a bet on the future rate of inflation. In the mid- to late-1980s redemption yields on bonds were higher than they had been historically in relation to inflation. If inflation was to stabilise around this level (below 5% per year), interest rates would eventually fall. That means that bonds will gain in price, as well as offering attractive coupon income. But the risk is ever-present that inflation will pick up again. In those circumstances bond investors will be hurt once again, as they have been for much of this century. Nominal interest rates will rise, bond prices will fall, and it would have been safer to have put your money in almost any other investment.

One route round this problem – and to my mind a potentially attractive one – is investment in index-linked bonds. They offer the same security as conventional bonds, but the added security that if inflation does pick up the owner will not lose out. There are very few other assets around about which you can say that!

c h a p t e r · *4*

*T*he · *s*hares · *m*arket ·

A share in the economy ·

Suppose that at the end of 1918 you, or one of your relatives, had bought shares in a variety of British companies with a total value of £1000. Suppose also that, in all the years since, you had been able to plough all the cash pay-outs (dividends) from those shares back into the total investment, and to avoid taxes. Your portfolio would now be worth over £2 million. Of course, £2 million doesn't buy what it used to: in terms of real purchasing power your £1000 would have turned into something like £125 000 in 1918 money. In other words, your wealth would have increased by a factor of more than 100 in the period since the end of the First World War.

This kind of outstanding long-run performance explains why there is so much interest in shares as an investment. This chapter looks at the general principles behind investment in shares, or 'equities' as they are known in financial parlance. It looks first at the share markets; then at the owners of shares and their rights; examines the long-run performance of shares as an investment in more detail; and goes into some of the key issues to be considered if you are to make money out of shares.

*T*he share markets ·

The UK share market is extremely large. The total market value of shares at the time of writing is close to £400 billion. That's a hard number to get into perspective, but some feeling for it may be got from the fact that it amounts to over £7000 for every person in the United Kingdom.

The world market in shares is much bigger still: it's something like ten times the size of the UK market. In capitalist countries the shares market is an absolutely vital asset market: it's the way in which individuals can benefit from the most dynamic wealth-creating forces in the economy. The long-run returns from shares reflect this dynamism. As a result, if you're keen that your money should make more money, it's almost certainly going to be sensible for you to take an interest in the shares market at some point.

The shareholders ·

Who owns shares? In the United Kingdom the largest proportion are owned by the 'institutions'. These are mainly insurance companies and pension funds. So even if you own no shares yourself directly, your future financial well-being may well depend on the shares market. Both your insurance company and your pension fund are probably very heavily invested in it.

Until the 1960s, wealthy private individuals played a major direct role in the shares market; then up until 1979 their role declined. There were two reasons for this: a decline in the relative wealth of the kind of people who were investors in the sixties and the relatively low returns from shares in the late sixties and early seventies. But since then new individual wealth has made a comeback in the market. At the end of 1987 the 'personal sector' owned UK shares worth £116 billion, around one-quarter of the market total.

Nine million investors

There have been two major factors at work in the return of the private shareholder. The first was the massive and sustained general rise in share prices between 1975 and 1987, which attracted much media and investor attention. The second has been the privatisation policy of the Conservative governments after 1979. The shares of the privatised companies were sold off at cheap prices in small lots; as was intended, this was a very tempting opportunity for millions of people. The net result is that at the time of writing there are something like nine million individual shareholders in the United Kingdom. Chapter 5 looks at the opportunities likely to be offered by future privatisations.

Shares and shareholders ·

What is a share? It is precisely what it says it is. The owner of a share in a company shares equally in the control and progress of that company. Each share carries one vote. In theory, at least, the shareholders control the direction of the company which they own. After all costs have been paid, including the costs of interest on loans from banks and the like, the remaining profits belong to the shareholders. They may vote to have the income which belongs to them paid out in the form of dividends, or retained and ploughed back into the company's future.

Owning one share entitles you to receive the annual dividend from that share. The dividend is normally paid out in cash in two separate instalments a year. To calculate the dividend you are owed, multiply the number of shares you own by the dividend per share. A shareholding of 100 shares will entitle you to 100 times the annual dividend, and so on. As a shareholder, you have the right to attend the annual general meeting of your company, to get its annual reports, and to receive its dividends. All shareholders have these rights.

Exercising shareholders' rights

One of the largest companies in the UK is Shell Transport and Trading. The companies which it controls include several which are active in South Africa. Shareholders in Shell Transport and Trading who were strongly opposed to apartheid in South Africa have disrupted the annual general meeting of Shell Transport and Trading for the last several years. They are fully within their rights in raising the issue of Shell's policy in South Africa in such meetings.

But most shareholders don't have political goals as such. In theory, at least, they do have control of the companies in which they own shares. The theory runs that shareholders control the direction of the companies in which they invest through the election of the directors of those companies. The directors in turn set the strategy of the company, and appoint the key managers who conduct its day-to-day operations.

Who runs companies?

How closely does this accord with what we observe in practice? The answer is: not very closely. Indeed, the logic often appears to be reversed in modern large companies. The senior managers of the company rise through the company's ranks; they effectively appoint the directors, who are often ex-senior managers of the company or other 'wise old men'. There are, at present, few women on the boards of UK companies, wise or not.

These directors effectively rubber-stamp the decisions that the senior managers want to take. This may seem reasonable: managers are, after all, professionals. However, they're also human; they're quite likely to have their own interests at heart. Those interests are not necessarily the interests of the shareholders. Managers generally gain prestige and salary from controlling a larger company, with higher sales and more employees; that's not necessarily the same thing as a more profitable company.

Distant directors

Why are the directors so distant from their shareholders? The major reason is simply the size of modern industry. At the time of writing, ICI has about 680 million shares outstanding. Each of those shares is worth about £10. The total value of ICI, therefore, is around £6800 million. Very few, if any, individuals have the sort of wealth that makes up even a small proportion of this total. Raising enough capital to finance large companies means having many investors. It simply isn't possible for all of them to be involved in decision-making.

It is logical for investors to turn to experts – that is, the senior managers of the company – to give guidance on how the company should be run and what its long-term objectives should be. However, the investor should remember that his or her own objectives are not necessarily quite the same as those of the managers.

There are two pieces of good news for shareholders, though. The first is that he or she always has the option to sell his or her shares. If he or she does not like the direction in which the company is going, he or she can always sell out to somebody else who's happier about it. The second is that, if managers are doing a very bad job, it will be profitable for someone else to come along and take over the company – normally at significant profit to the existing shareholders.

Returns from shares ·

We've already looked at returns over the very long period from 1918. Those returns are equivalent to an average rate of just over 7% per year in real terms (after allowing for the effects of inflation). So in the very long run the investor who put £100 into the stock market at the start of a year could on average expect to get just over £107 back, in terms of real purchasing power, at the end of that year.

Recent returns

This is also approximately true over more recent periods. Since the end of 1945 the real return has been just over 6% per year. That means that £1000 invested at the end of 1945 had turned, by the end of 1987, into around £12 500 in real terms.

The record over some shorter periods is better still. Over the ten years between the end of 1977 and the end of 1987 the average return was almost 12% per annum in real terms. We'll see below why this rate of return could not be sustained in the long term. Investors who got into shares in the mid-1970s did very well, especially if they also managed to get out again just before the October 1987 crash! However, those who came to believe that boom-market returns could be expected every year were dangerously deluded.

Beware of the average · · ·

The data used here comes from the *Equity-Gilt Study* by Barclays de Zoete Wedd (BZW), a firm of stockbrokers. They have been used to calculate the returns quoted above. BZW present data collected over a long period of time which are calculated using 'indices'. Indices measure average share-market behaviour (indices are explained in Chapter 6).

It's important to realise that the performance of individual shares can differ hugely from the average, over any period. Some of the companies in existence at the time the records start are no longer in existence – they were taken over, or perhaps even went bankrupt. Other small companies grew massively in value, and eventually became the giant companies around us today. But it's still important to look at the long-term pattern of share-market behaviour.

Since the market is very volatile, only a long history can provide a realistic picture of the kind of returns that we can expect, taking one year – or one decade – with another. The past is the best guide that we have to what the future will be like, although it obviously isn't perfect.

One very bad aspect of the UK's equity market boom at the end of the 1980s was the media focus on just the very good short-term performance record. The result was that some people got the erroneous belief that shares contain very little risk and offer extremely high returns. It's not going too far to say that they were 'suckered into' the marketplace: in the unluckiest cases, just in time for 'Black Monday' and the Crash of October 1987.

Tax

All the returns from shares quoted so far are before tax. But most investors cannot avoid tax in one form or another. So from the end of 1945, if our notional investor had been paying basic-rate income tax, his £1000 would have grown not to £12 500 but only to £5800. This is still a substantial gain: instead of an increase in value of over 6% per year in real terms, his portfolio increased in value by just over 4% per year in real terms after tax.

The importance of dividends ·

While media attention is focused on movements in the price of shares, the real story that matters to the long-term investor is less glamorous. Most people probably think of stock-market gains as coming mainly from increases in the price of shares ('capital appreciation'). That's because in the five years up to October 1987 this was the case. However, the long-term record reveals something very different.

The real return from owning a varied bundle ('diversified portfolio') of shares over the period since the end of 1945 has averaged just over 6% per year; of that 6% only just over 1% per year has come from increases in the capital price of shares. Where has the other 5% come from? The answer is from the annual flow, and reinvestment of, dividends. Dividends are cash pay-outs to shareholders by companies from their profits each year. The ratio of the annual dividend to the value of a share is known as its dividend yield. In the long run dividends provide most of the gain which shareholders get from owning shares.

Dividends return the most

Movements in the price of shares only just outpace inflation. The important return from owning shares is from the dividends that are paid out each year, and which with luck will go on growing over time. The total contribution of dividends to the returns from most greatly exceeds that from price increases ('capital appreciation').

This makes sense when we think about the source of increases in the price of shares. Shares are a stake in the prosperity of the British economy. The economy is growing as managers and workers become more productive. In most years it gets bigger in real terms, but it doesn't grow very quickly. Over the long run, it's growing at about 2% or 3% a year.

This limits the rate of increase in average share prices. All shares taken together are 'deeds of ownership' of total UK company profits, and therefore in the British economy. Their value too will grow at around 2 to 3% per year in real terms. As the economy evolves, shares in small fast-growing companies will increase in value by a bit more than this average rate; shares in large established companies will tend to increase by a bit less than the average.

Because the economy is growing only moderately, the real capital value of shares can only grow relatively slowly. And the only other source of income from holding shares is dividends.

Risk and return ·

A return from shares of about 6% per year in real terms, although it's not as dramatic as some people may have been led to expect, is well in excess of that offered by most other types of investment. The reason for this is, broadly, that shares also offer a high degree of risk. Because of this risk investors are only prepared to hold shares if they offer a reasonable promise of return. Some of the time the return doesn't come through, in fact, the shareholder can lose a large amount of wealth. That's the risk! It follows that when the return does come through it has to be reasonably large.

There is a trade-off between risk and return. If shares were safer investors would be happier to hold them. The price of shares would be higher. However, dividend payments would remain unchanged, so the result would be that shares would offer a lower dividend yield, and a lower total return. In fact, prices would rise until the lower expected return just balanced the lower risk level. On the other hand, if investors believed that shares were becoming very risky, they would try to sell out and would bid down the price of those shares. An investor at the lower prices could expect a higher return. At some point the higher expected return would pay investors enough for taking on the higher risk.

Risk

In this section we look at the risks an investor would have run in the past by owning a diversified portfolio of shares (once again the data come from BZW). The risks involved in having money in the shares of just one or two companies are usually much higher; there's more about this in Chapter 5.

Of the 42 separate years between the end of 1945 and the end of 1987, the investor in a diversified portfolio of UK shares lost money, after inflation was taken into account, in 18. That's about four years out of every ten. (The four-in-ten ratio is also roughly true of the much longer period since the end of the First World War.) Some of the bad years were much worse than others: in seven out of the 18 'down' years between 1945 and 1987, the real value of a portfolio fell by more than 10%. That's a sizeable loss of real wealth.

The worse year since the First World War for share investors was 1974. An investment in shares at the end of 1973 would have lost 57.5% – well over half – of its real value over the next 12 months. As it happens this terrible year came immediately after the second-worst year on record. Someone unfortunate enough to invest in shares at the end of 1972 would have lost 74% – three-quarters – of the real value of their investment over the course of the next two years! The total decline of share values between 1972 and 1974 was, in fact, far worse than that experienced by investors during the crash of October 1987.

The point of these stories of disaster is not to frighten you away from shares. It is to hammer home that owning even a diversified portfolio of shares is not for the faint-hearted, or for those who must have their money back at a certain time. It really can be a risky business.

The Crashes of 1973–4 and 1987

Many people are put off from investing in shares by the possibility of another 'crash'. There are two episodes of very sharp declines in share prices in recent British history. The first occurred during 1973 and 1974, and the second – in a much shorter period of time – in October 1987.

The first crash involved larger losses of real wealth than the second, although it was less spectacular. Prices fell steadily for long periods of time in 1973–4. There was no one-day equivalent to 'Black Monday', 19 October 1987, when prices plunged in shares markets around the world.

Another important difference between 1973–4 and 1987 was that in the first period the rate of inflation was high and getting higher – it finally peaked at almost 27% in September 1975. Oil prices quadrupled in late 1973, and militant trade unions were winning very large wage increases for their members. Rising inflation contributed to the loss of confidence that drove down share prices (for example, some people thought that it might lead to the end of capitalism in Britain), and of course it was devouring the real value of any fixed amount of money. The loss of real wealth in shares was due not just to share prices falling, but to rising prices of everything else. This wasn't happening to a significant extent in 1987.

However, there were also similarities between the two episodes. It is instructive to list some of them.

1973–4	1987
Booming economy until summer 1974	Booming economy
Rising interest rates	Rising interest rates
Conservative government until March 1974	Conservative government
Very low dividend yields before crash	Very low dividend yields before crash

It's easy to see why rising interest rates, which make fixed-income investments more attractive, are bad for shares. However, some of the other common features are at first sight surprising. Booming economies are good for company profits, and so might be expected to be good for shares. Similarly Conservative governments are usually thought of as good for the shares market.

The reason for this paradox is that the shares market tries to anticipate, not what is happening right now, but what's going to happen next year or the year after. If there are good times now the market fears there may be bad times just around the corner. The greater the optimism today – the greater the potential fall tomorrow.

Risk and time

Risk reduces with the length of the time you're prepared to hold the shares. Over very long periods, the risk of actually losing money by holding a diversified portfolio of shares is very low. For example, the investor would not have lost money in any of the separate 25-year periods since the First World War (for example, 1963–87 inclusive). The worst you would have managed was a real return of 2.7% per year, enough to turn a £1000 original investment into £1950 (the best 25-year return was 10.2% per year, which would have turned £1000 into £11 300).

For shorter periods the risk of losing money increases. In eight of the 38 'five-year' periods between 1945 and 1987 (1945–50, 1946–51 and so on) investors in shares lost money after allowing for inflation. But that's only about two in ten, compared with losses in about four in every ten individual years.

The table below gives an estimate of the chances of losing, or making, different amounts of money from investment in UK shares over periods of different length. This table is based on share performance since the end of the First World War. It assumes that the investor bought a representative portfolio of shares but had no special investment strategy. While there's no guarantee that the future will be just like the past, the table is the best available guide to the likely future pattern of risks.

Investment period	Chance (%) of:			
	Losing at least 20%	Losing at all	Making at least 50%	Doubling money
1 year	11	38	8	*
2 years	14	34	21	5
5 years	11	23	45	14
10 years	5	10	70	50
20 years	*	*	97	91

Sources: BZW, author. * = chance of less than 0.5% (1 in 200).

For example, the table implies that if you invest in shares and hold on to them for ten years, reinvesting all the dividends, there is a 70% (seven-in-ten) chance that you will enjoy a total real return of at least 50% on your investment.

Summing up

While there's always a risk that you'll lose money in shares, it diminishes with the length of time you're willing to hold the shares. That's one of the reasons why shares are a very popular investment with insurance companies and pension funds. They face 'long-term liabilities', such as pensions that they'll have to pay out many years from now; what they're looking for is good long-run performance, and they're prepared to accept the odd poor year on the basis of that good performance. Shares are a natural asset for such investors.

They are also a natural asset for you, if you've got a long time horizon. But it's vital that you know your own preferences. If you're going to need the money tomorrow shares are not for you; you'd be far better off putting your money in the building society. However, if you can wait for five, ten or 20 years – and you can cope emotionally with some large bumps along the way – then shares are likely to give you a far better return.

The next section looks at one possible way of reducing the risk of investing in the shares market. The discussion of risk above was based on the assumption that the investor is neither good nor bad at timing his or her dealings in shares. It just may be possible to do better than that – if you're tough-minded enough to buy when all looks black, and to sell again when all looks rosy.

Timing the market? ·

I believe that you may be able to get slightly better-than-average results in the UK shares market by following a simple method. The emphases in the last sentence are on the words 'may' and 'slightly'. As you'll see, this area is controversial. You'll also see that, even if the method is of some use, it certainly doesn't take all the risk out of investing in shares.

Academics take a walk

Many academic experts believe that the prices of individual shares, and of the shares market as a whole, follow what is called a 'random walk', and that there is no way of telling if the next move in the shares market will be up or down. (There is an excellent investment book called *A Random Walk down Wall Street*, by Burton Malkiel, an American academic.) The random walk idea is usually associated with the Efficient Markets Theory. This is less forbidding than it sounds.

The basic idea is that thousands of competitive and intelligent investors just like you make sure that anything that can be known that is at all relevant to the price of a share – new products, interest rates, profit levels, or anything else – will rapidly be reflected in the price of that share. What's true of one share is true of all shares taken together. So no form of analysis should be able to help you predict what the share market will do next. Only 'news', that is new information which no one can anticipate, can move the market.

So, as no one can predict the news, no one can predict the next move in the market. It could equally as well be up as down.

Attractive theory slain by ugly fact

The theory is attractive. However, at least in the case of the overall UK shares market over the last 40 years, it is just not consistent with the facts. Look at the chart opposite.

The chart shows that, since 1946, a high dividend yield on the overall market has been a good predictor of a subsequent high return. When dividend yields are low, shares have tended to do badly over the next 12 months.

Each point on the chart stands for a separate calendar year. There are 42 points, one for each of the years 1946 to 1987 inclusive. The closer the point to the right-hand edge of the chart, the higher was the dividend yield of the FT All-Share index (described in more detail on page 127) at the start of that year. The closer the point to the top edge of the chart, the higher was the total real return from shares over the next 12 months.

The points on the right-hand side also tend to be higher up. Although the 'fit' is far from perfect, a formal statistical test shows that there is virtually no chance that this connection between dividend yields at the start of the year and total real returns during that year could have arisen by accident.

The lone point in the top right-hand corner shows the very high returns from shares during 1975, plotted against the extremely high average dividend yield at the start of that year. Although this unusual year does emphasise the connection, it is far from being the only reason for it – there is still a strong link even if 1975 is ignored. What the chart shows is that you could have used the average dividend yield at the start of the year to 'predict' what would happen to shares during the next 12 months. The market has not taken a random walk.

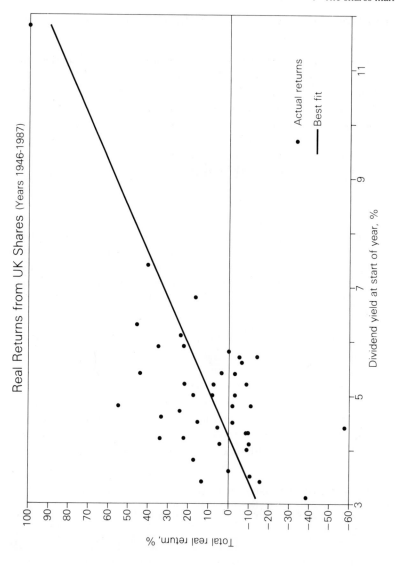

Real Returns from UK Shares (Years 1946-1987)

to shares during the next 12 months. The market has not taken a random walk.

You would have done even better by including the inflation rate over the past year as an additional guide to what shares were going to do. High inflation during one year has usually been bad for returns from shares during the next year. This may be because it's been linked to rising costs which companies can't pass on fully into prices. So profits suffer.

Why not a random walk?

This finding puts us in much the same position as the economist who is supposed to have said: 'This works in practice, but does it work in theory?' I can only suggest my own explanation of why dividend yields have actually been good predictors of future returns. Neither the chart nor the explanation are in widespread use yet amongst either academics or City professionals (although Gavyn Davies and Sushil Wadhwani, writing for the investment bank Goldman Sachs, did notice the same pattern in the same historical data independently).

Investors influence each other. Crowds are capable of believing and doing things that most of their individual members, on their own, would never believe or do. So it seems reasonable to believe that there are peaks and troughs of market 'emotion' which carry the general level of share prices too high or too low at individual moments in time. This is obviously true looking at history: there are times when with hindsight it would have been good to buy, and other times when it would have been good to sell. The trick is to identify these points at the time – and ignore the herd.

The key point here is that one good measure of underlying market value is the total flow of all dividends from all shares to shareholders.

A low dividend yield means that shares are more likely to perform poorly over the course of the next year. This is because the optimism that pervades the market has pushed prices very high, and so has driven the ratio of dividends to prices (the dividend yield) to a low level. Eventually investors will become more pessimistic. At that point prices will fall in relation to dividends. The average dividend yield will begin to climb towards, and perhaps beyond, more normal levels.

When pessimism is all-pervasive, average dividend yield will be high and it becomes more likely that the next period will be a good one in which to be in shares. Eventually sentiment recovers. Then prices rise again, reducing dividend yields towards their more normal level.

Mr Market runs riot

Benjamin Graham, a famous and very successful American investor, made much the same point when he compared owning shares to being in a business partnership with a manic-depressive called 'Mr Market'. Every day Mr Market offers you a price at which you have the chance either to buy his share of the business off him, or to sell your share of the business to him. On most days you can and should ignore his offer. Just occasionally he will either offer such a good price that you ought to sell; or is so depressed that he asks such a low price that you ought to buy.

In the summer of 1987 average dividend yields had fallen to their lowest level in modern times. In other words, share prices were very high relative to the underlying flow of dividends from those shares. These prices might have been sensible if Nirvana had arrived. In this Nirvana dividends would grow rapidly and safely for ever for all companies. Therefore, very high share prices in relation to today's dividends would be justified. However, history tells us that Nirvana has never arrived. Eventually something will come along that will change the public mood. In October 1987 what arrived was a growing belief that share prices had risen much too far relative to realistic expectations about the course of the world economy. The correction, when it came, was savage – both in Britain and around the world.

Investors who followed the type of 'dividend model' of share market performance represented in the chart on page 89 would have kept out of the market in September 1987. Therefore, they could have avoided the crash . . . In practice they would have found it very difficult to do so. The model would also have told them to be out of the market for many months before the crash occurred. As those months went by, investors who followed the model's advice would have felt more and more foolish as prices soared around them. Other investors were reaping profits.

It was possible to believe – and many investors did believe – that the shares market was much safer under Conservative governments. Others thought that Japanese investors, used to even lower dividend yields in the domestic Japanese share market, were becoming a dominant force in the British market; and that they would continue to buy the shares of UK companies even at yields which seemed very low to British investors.

THE CRASH OF '87...

Herds of nerds

We now know that none of these factors had permanently broken the link between dividends and prices. However, it would have taken iron discipline to stay out of the market in these circumstances. One of the strongest instincts is the herd instinct – most of us would prefer to be wrong in company, than alone and right.

Predicting future returns

Just for fun, let's look at what the historical link between dividend yield and total real return 'predicts' at various dividend yields. The table below shows these 'predictions'. It is simply the 'best fit' line from the chart on page 95, shown as a table.

Dividend yield on FT All-Share index %:	3	3.5	4	4.5	5	5.5	6	7
'Predicted' return % from chart best fit:	−15	−9	−3	3	9	15	21	33

For example, at the time of writing in late 1988, the dividend yield on the *Financial Times* All-Share index is just under 4.4%. On the basis of the chart, the 'predicted' total real return from the average share over the next year is just below 2%.

It must be stressed that these predictions should not be taken too seriously. They are just the best very simple guesses, based on the experience since the Second World War. The future may be very different from the past. Also the chart shows that even over the past, the 'best fit' was a long way from perfect. Returns from shares for individual years vary widely from the line! However, an investor who did believe in this kind of analysis would not be heavily invested in shares at the time of writing. If the best guess is that shares won't give a very high return, there's not much point in exposing one's money to the risk that they'll go down sharply. The investor would be better off with his or her money in the building society.

If the dividend yield was to rise to, for example, 5%, the prospects for shares for our investor would begin to become more interesting. Such a rise in yields can come about in one of two ways. Either share prices can fall further or dividends can rise. We know that dividends rise over time; therefore, even if average share prices don't move for a time, dividend yields tend to rise. When that happens, the chart suggests, it may be time to invest.

For the mathematically inclined

The chart implies that the relationship between the total real return from UK shares in each of the years 1946 to 1987 and the All-Share dividend yield at the start of each year can be expressed as an equation:

Real return in % = −50.3 + 11.9 × Yield

This equation 'explains' 41% of the overall variation in real returns.

It was mentioned on page 90 that including the inflation rate over the past year, in addition to the dividend yield, led to even closer predictions of the real returns from shares. This regression equation is:

Real return in % = −58.1 + 16.0 × Yield − 2.0 × Inflation

This version explains 53% of the variation in real returns.

Think long-term

Does timing your entry or exit to the shares market really matter in the long run? Obviously it can affect your results significantly. The chart opposite offers some evidence of this. It's like the chart in the previous section, except that it compares average annual real returns from shares over ten-year periods with the dividend yield from the All-Share index at the start of each ten-year period. Although the link between starting dividend yield and subsequent returns isn't as strong as with the one-year returns, it's still noticeable. If history is a guide, it's usually better even for long-term investors in shares to invest when dividend yields are high (if they can!). However, don't dwell on this point for too long. It's much more important for you to realise that you'll probably make money in shares if you just hold onto them for long enough.

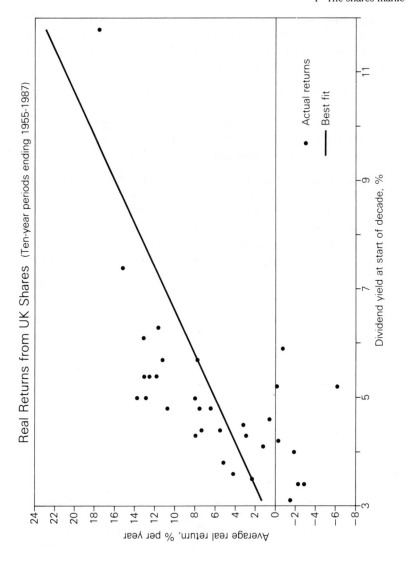

Real Returns from UK Shares (Ten-year periods ending 1955-1987)

Average real return, % per year

Dividend yield at start of decade, %

• Actual returns

—— Best fit

Longer-term investors tend to make money almost whenever they invest. The chart confirms this. It shows that real returns were positive in the great majority of ten-year periods. What's more, the 'predicted' real return over ten years is positive even when dividend yields are very low.

If you are thinking of making a long-term investment in the shares market, timing your entry is less important than having the commitment to seeing your investments through. In the end, they'll almost certainly come up trumps. The problem is just that there will probably be large 'bumps' along the way. You've got to be prepared to ride these out.

This chapter has dealt with the returns and risks from the shares market as a whole. An investor would only obtain these returns, and face these risks, if he or she owned a widely-diversified portfolio of shares (in other words, a well-spread mixture of shares in different companies). Real life usually isn't like this. In practice you don't 'buy the market' but individual shares. Chapter 5 looks at the key factors to bear in mind when deciding on which shares to choose.

Investing · in · individual · shares ·

This chapter considers some of the points to bear in mind when investing in shares in individual companies. You'll see that three of the steps to success-ful investing mentioned in Chapter 1 – diversifying, hunting for value, and not over-trading – are of particular importance.

Individual share risk ·

All the evidence about risk and return discussed in the previous chapter relates to the share market as a whole. In practice you don't buy 'the market'. You buy shares in specific companies. The important point here is that the shares of a specific company are almost always considerably more risky than the market as a whole.

Most shares go up and down with the general level of the whole market, at least to some extent. If prospects for the whole economy improve most indi-vidual shares will go up as well: most companies will be set to share in the increased general prosperity. However, even if the market as a whole does well, a share in a specific company may plummet – and vice versa. The reason is that things may happen to the company which are unrelated to the general economic scene: it may launch a successful new product, or be taken over, or lose a key executive, or face a damaging strike, or . . .

On the other hand, the average of shares can only offer the same return that the market as a whole offers. The trick is to 'pick winners' – and this chapter will try to help you on your way – but it's only realistic to suppose that you won't do much better than the market average.

One-company portfolios are riskiest

So if you invest in the shares of only one company you can probably expect a level of return close to that from the whole market. That's the best guess. However, this return carries a much higher level of risk. There will be much more variation in the return from month to month, or year to year, than there would be if you owned many different shares. The fewer shares you own the more philosophical you need to be about their peaks and troughs.

Many different factors influence the riskiness of individual shares. Some important ones are: the industry the company is in, the financial structure of the company, and – particularly – its size. A detailed analysis is beyond the scope of this book. However, even for a large company share risk (the variability of returns) is usually much greater than that of the market as a whole.

Spread the risk

Therefore, unless you're a gambler by nature, it's a good idea to 'diversify' your holdings: spread them across several different shares. What's good for ICI may be bad for British Telecom, and have no effect whatsoever on Shell. By spreading your holdings you can greatly reduce the risks of your overall investment in shares.

Diversification versus costs

Having small amounts of money in the shares of many different companies would be an excellent way of diversifying risk. Unfortunately, it's not a very good idea. There are two main reasons. It presents the investor with the need to 'follow' lots of different companies, but the much more important reason is cost.

The normal way to buy or sell shares (other than 'new issues', such as most of the privatisation issues, which can be bought directly using published application forms) is through someone with access to a 'market-maker' in shares. That's usually a stockbroker or another financial institution, for example a bank. They charge you for providing this service. The problem with small share deals is that they cost the stockbroker or bank just as much to process as larger ones. So most have now adopted a minimum charge. This varies from firm to firm – it's worth shopping around – but at the time of writing a typical minimum is about £25 (plus VAT!) per deal.

Big is beautiful

This minimum charge clearly has a much bigger effect on the overall return from buying, holding and selling a small investment in a share than its effect on a large investment. For example, £25-plus-VAT (£28.75 in total) is equal to 14.4% of a £200 investment; to 5.75% of a £500 investment; and to 2.9% of a £1000 investment. For larger investments the minimum charge is usually replaced by a percentage rate, but it's almost always the case that the percentage cost of dealing in shares is lower, the larger the deal that you want to do.

We saw in Chapter 4 that the long-term average real return from shares was of the order of 6 or 7% per year. So, on a £500 holding, dealing charges on the purchase alone can come close to wiping out a typical year's return! Of course you also have to pay dealing charges when you finally sell your shares. This combination is a large drag on the overall return from your investment unless you hold it for a very long time.

A grand recommendation

Holding small investments in many different shares can seriously damage your returns. Because of this, I recommend that, except in special circumstances (for example, because a privatisation allows you to deal more cheaply than usual), you aim to hold not less than about £1000 worth of shares in any one company. This obviously poses problems if you don't have huge amounts to put into shares. Minimum dealing charges make it attractive to concentrate your holdings in a very few shares; but this will mean that you don't get the risk-reducing benefits of diversification.

*U*nit and investment trusts ·

There is no magic solution to this problem. One not entirely satisfactory way of side-stepping it is to buy into a unit trust or investment trust instead of buying shares for yourself directly. Both sorts of trust are large 'pools' of money managed by professionals who invest it in shares or other securities. Your investment buys a small share of the total portfolio.

Because a trust can and typically does invest in many different shares, your investment in it will be diversified. The extent of the diversification depends on the trust. A 'general UK equity' trust will usually perform roughly in line with the whole market. It will be much less risky than one which invests solely in, say, small computer companies, or Australian gold mines.

Don't entirely trust the trusts

There are three main reasons why buying into a trust is not entirely satisfactory:

1   You lose the pleasure of controlling your own investments.

2   The returns achieved by many trusts are not particularly inspiring. The investment judgement shown by the managers of many trusts may well be no better than, or worse than, your own. There is, unfortunately, no reliable way

of distinguishing ahead of time trusts which will do well from those which will do badly!

3   The charges levied by trusts can be substantial. Buying shares in investment trusts is just like buying any other share, with similar dealing costs. When buying units in a unit trust it is quite usual to pay an initial charge of 5% or more of the value of your investment. In addition, you will pay an annual management fee of, typically, 0.5–1.5% each year.

In the end, the attractions of unit and investment trusts to some extent depend on temperament. 'Know yourself'! If you have only a small amount to put into shares (less than £5000, say) you should certainly consider trusts unless you are prepared to take large risks. If you are very concerned to control risk or have little interest in managing your own portfolio of shares, trusts may be attractive.

If you decide to put money into a unit trust or investment trust, take care to find out about its general features before you invest. Different trusts focus on different investments – for example, some feature shares which are expected to grow in value over the long term, others shares which provide a higher dividend yield now, and others individual sectors or foreign markets. Before you invest you should know about the areas in which a trust specialises, and about its past performance record. This information is available in, for example, the monthly magazine *Money Management*, which provides consistent information on the comparative records of the unit trusts in different categories over different time periods.

The rest of this chapter looks at some of the main issues to think about if you're going to make the decision about which shares to invest in yourself. You need some way of deciding which shares to buy!

*B*eating the market ·

Professional investors realise that, because the shares market is highly competitive, it's difficult to outperform the market indices (see page 88). But many investment professionals, like Sir John Templeton, believe that it is possible to beat the market by searching continually for shares which other investors have neglected. Through the market's ignorance of their potential these shares are available at bargain prices. The key to outperforming the index is therefore to find shares that are selling for below their true value.

Valuing shares ·

But what is the true value of a share? One answer is a rather obvious and trivial one: the value of something is what it would cost you to buy it in the market-place. Therefore the value of a share is the price of that share in today's market. Of course, that definition doesn't help the investor who's trying to beat the market. What he or she means by value is something rather different. Value to the professional investor is the 'fair' price at which he or she thinks the share in question ought to sell, given normal market circumstances. It's the price which a logical market which shared the investor's own views about the future would arrive at.

The easiest way long-term investors can put their own value on a share is to arrive at their own guess of what that share will return over future years in dividends.

Desperately seeking dividends

Dividends are cash payments to the shareholders, made usually once or twice a year, in proportion to the number of shares they own. The dividend level is decided on by the company's directors. In looking for shares to buy, anticipating the future flow of dividends from a share is the single most important concern the long-term investor should have.

There may or may not be dividends from a company's shares at present. Many young or fast-growing companies choose to plough all their profits back into the further expansion of the company. Even well-established companies will sometimes follow this practice. Digital Equipment Corporation, a large US computer company, is one example.

This does not mean that the shares of Digital Equipment, or of other companies which do not now pay dividends, are valueless. What it does mean is that investors in these companies must hope that the eventual payment of dividends will justify their present investment. The same is true for investors who hold shares in companies which are not paying dividends because they have fallen on hard times and are not presently making profits with which to pay dividends.

How to value future dividends

Whether a company pays dividends now or not, it is the 'expectation' of the future flow of dividends that determines the value of its shares for the long-term investor. A dividend received far in the future is of less value to the investor than one which is received today. There are two reasons for this.

In the first place, if the dividend is received today it can be invested in a safe, fixed-income asset which yields a guaranteed return, like a building society account. Present dividends are therefore worth more than future ones; future dividends cannot gain interest in the building society as from tomorrow.

In the second place, tomorrow's dividend is 'uncertain'. The investor cannot be sure that the company will be in a position to pay the expected dividend in one year's time, in ten years' time, or further into the future. Indeed, the further away the expected dividend, the less certain it becomes.

Take account – then discount

The wise investor proceeds with a great deal of caution in these circum-stances. He or she will pay a lower price for, or 'discount', the expected value of future dividends. Today's bird in the hand is worth two birds in a future bush.

The price is right?

The theory is clear, then. The fair value of a share is the expected future flow of dividends from that share, suitably discounted. But when we say this, we reveal exactly how difficult the process of getting at fair value really is. We have first of all to predict what future dividends will be, each year, for all time! Then we have to work out a discount factor to apply to those dividends – the discount factor has to reflect both that future dividends are not earning inter-est for us now and the risk that they may not arrive at all.

Expected dividends and the discount factor to apply to them are linked. Usually if we expect the dividends of a company to grow very fast those divi-dends will also be highly uncertain. Who can be really sure the company will actually live up to investors' expectations? As a result, the expected divi-dends from that company's shares will tend to be heavily discounted.

How professionals spot an investment opportunity ·

Some of the investment professionals who work for sophisticated investing institutions do really use this 'dividend discount model' in making their decisions. They work out fair values for a large number of different shares, and then invest in those where the actual price is the farthest below this fair value.

But the complexity of the dividend discount model puts it beyond the scope of the average private investor. Instead, many professionals and most private investors use a number of short-cut methods. They see if the current share price is high or low compared with some simple measures that give a rough clue as to its fair value. The ultimate objective is the same as that of the dividend discount model. However, the indicators used are much easier to calculate.

Simple indicators

To find out about a company and predict its future performance you need to be able to make some sense of its accounts. These are published annually – and include the raw data you will need to get your own idea of a company's true value. The owner of shares in a company is sent the accounts automatically. If you are not a shareholder, most companies will send you copies of their latest accounts if you write to them (write to the Company Secretary at the company's registered office, which can be found in directories which should be available at your local library). Some newspapers and magazines will also provide copies of the most recent accounts of companies in which you are particularly interested. Earnings and dividend figures are available every day in the shares pages of newspapers (as is explained in Chapter 6).

As you turn the pages of the annual accounts you will find figures for the following key measures of a company's value:

Net Assets (also known as Book Value)

All companies employ assets to do whatever it is that they do. True assets are things which last a long time and which can be used in the productive process. They can be anything from a steel mill to a highly-skilled advertising director. 'Book' assets appear in the 'balance sheet' section of a company's accounts. However, these assets are often only a small part of total true assets. Book assets are almost entirely physical in nature: the steel mill is in the accounts, the advertising director isn't – the company doesn't own him.

Assets get into the accounts when the company first buys them and are valued at whatever the company paid for them in that year. Thereafter they are depreciated: this means that a proportion of their value is subtracted each year, as they decay or become obsolete.

Suppose a company purchased an oil refinery in 1965 for £10 million. It might be decided at the time that the asset should be written off ('depreciated') over 20 years. That means that its net value in the accounts was reduced by half a million pounds every year until 1985, when it was deemed to be of no value at all. This might well be a nonsense. In the first place the oil refinery might have many years of life left in it; in the second place it would be impossible to replace it for anything like the value carried in the books. On the other hand, the refinery might indeed now be of no value – it might be obsolete, or the demand for oil might have fallen so far that it would no longer be profitable to operate the refinery. The point of this example is to show that the book value – the accounting value – of any asset may bear very little relation to its true economic value. Nevertheless, total book value is still often the best measure that we have of the productive assets under a company's control.

To get at the assets which belong to the shareholders, we deduct the debts ('liabilities') which the company owes – remember that the shareholders are the 'residual' owners of the company, after all debts have been paid. We then work out the value of these assets per share. The higher the net assets per share in relation to the price of that share, the better buy is the share.

A real-life example

The total assets of the electronics company Plessey on 1 April 1988 (the end of Plessey's 1987–8 financial year) were £1291.6 million. However, Plessey also had short-term debts (for example, money owed to suppliers) of £488.6 million and long-term debts of £180.5 million. So the net assets belonging to the shareholders (called 'shareholders' funds' in the Plessey accounts) totalled £622.5 million. All of this information is shown on the balance sheet in the accounts.

Plessey had issued 741.5 million shares.

So, net assets per share were £622.5 million ÷ 741.5 = £0.840 or 84.0 pence.

Same shares have same snares

Even if the asset value carried on a company's balance sheet is not a good measure of true economic value it may still be the case that the accounts of different companies in the same industry contain the same kinds of distortions. Therefore if the true economic assets of company A are twice their book value, it's a fair bet that the true economic assets of company B – in the same industry – are also around twice their book value. Thus comparing the ratio of price to book value across different companies in the same business may give us a reasonable indication of relative value, even if it is a poor guide to absolute value. (Incidentally, we do not suggest that any of these hypotheses apply to Plessey.)

Raiders of the lost asset

One use of the indicator is in the case of takeovers. If a company's existing managers are not using assets efficiently, this could be reflected in a low ratio of the price of the shares to net asset value. A corporate raider, spotting this gap, could come along and buy the shares up. In this case the investor who had purchased the shares on the basis of the low ratio of price to book value could benefit from a high takeover price. This has been an important component of stock-market profits in the last few years. The raider pays a high price because he is betting that he can make the assets 'perform'.

Sales

Companies make sales, of course. Thus another guide to value is the level of sales per share. This gives us some idea of the 'franchise' which we are buying into when we buy a share. Everything else being equal, a company with more sales per share will offer better value. A low ratio of share price to sales per share suggests a good investment.

Plessey's sales for 1987–8 can be found in the 'profit and loss' section of the accounts. Sales, called 'turnover', totalled £1300.9 million for the year. So sales per share were £1300.9 million ÷ 741.5 million = £1.754 or 175.4 pence.

As yet the sales-based approach to value has found most favour in the United States, but it is likely that it will increasingly be used in the UK. It can be misleading, of course: a supermarket chain will have a very high level of sales per share, but it may be unable to convert those sales into profits because it makes so little profit on each item it sells. On the other hand, the sales of a pharmaceutical company per share may be rather low, but because of a highly profitable product line, perhaps, profits per share may be relatively high. When comparing these two companies, sales per share would not necessarily be a good guide as to which share offered better value. As in the price-to-book-value approach, the indicator is perhaps most powerful when used to compare companies in similar businesses.

Cash flow

Cash flow per share is the amount of money per share that the company is generating before it begins to think about replacing the assets that it has used up in the process. It is the amount that an owner could take out of the company if he or she was simply running it down, giving no thought to the preservation of the company. So it is not the same as profits.

Cash flow has not yet had 'depreciation' deducted from it. Assets really do wear out, so the best measure of a company's profits would take account of this true depreciation. However, we saw above that the depreciation numbers which actually appear in accounts are often arbitrary, and are usually prepared on the basis that an asset today costs the same as it cost when it was originally bought. Neither feature is at all helpful. It follows that in converting cash flow to earnings (profits) after depreciation, accountants are playing a form of Russian roulette. They may, or may not, help us to reach a better picture of a company's true profits.

For this reason, some investors prefer to look at cash flow per share before they look at profits. This is at best only a starting point in assessing the relative value of different shares. However, it is much used by some international investors in comparing shares between countries with very different accounting rules.

Working out cash flow

You won't find something called 'cash flow' in companies' accounts. Experts have differing views about what the precise definition ought to be. The simplest way to work out a version of cash flow is just to add depreciation to earnings after tax. Depreciation can be found in the 'sources and uses of funds' section of company accounts.

In our Plessey example, depreciation in 1987–8 was £63.3 million. Adding this back to earnings of £131.1 million (from the profit and loss section) gives cash flow of £194.4 million. That works out to 26.2 pence per share.

Earnings

Earnings are the 'official' estimate of what a company could return to share-holders if the existing business is to be maintained but not increased in size. All company accounts report both earnings and earnings per share. For Plessey in 1987–8 earnings were £131.1 million and earnings per share 17.7 pence. (Plessey also reports slightly lower figures for earnings and earnings per share 'before extraordinary items' – this year it generated some profits from an unusual source which did not arise from its normal business activities.)

Earnings per share are sometimes quoted as a percentage of the share price, a value known as the earnings yield. The more usual approach is to divide the share price by earnings per share to get the price-to-earnings (P/E) ratio. Because the P/E ratio is published in the shares pages of newspapers (see Chapter 6), you don't need a company's accounts to work out what its most recent year's earnings were.

Price/Earnings

The P/E ratio is probably the indicator of value best known amongst investors. It is often known as the 'multiple'. Multiples are frequently compared between firms in the same industry, and also across industries. The lower the ratio of price to earnings, the better the bargain the investor appears to be getting: he is having to pay less for each pound of profits.

This is not the whole story. Quite clearly, earnings which are stable or rapidly growing should be valued more highly than those which are unstable or falling. What is a very high multiple in one industry – say, banking – might be relatively low in another – for example, pharmaceuticals.

Dividends

Earnings are not the end of the story, however. Even if earnings per share are a good measure of the ongoing profitability of a company, there is still a problem for the investor.

The dividends paid to shareholders come out of the earnings. But managers control what is done with earnings. There is no requirement that the managers of the company pay out any particular proportion of earnings to the shareholders. Some managers will choose to pay no dividends at all – as is often the case with young, fast-growing companies. Other companies have less potential; nevertheless their managers may still try to make such companies bigger or more prestigious, so they choose to spend earnings on investment in unprofitable ventures, rather than return them to the shareholders.

It is hard to interpret some oil companies' use of their large profits in the late 1970s and early 1980s in any other way. Making large profits as a result of the higher price of oil, they chose not to return the money to the shareholders but to invest in companies and projects of which they knew little. The most spectacular examples were the takeovers of large metals companies by some oil companies.

The goals of senior managers in these oil companies seem to have been to make their companies as large as possible, and their own jobs as secure as possible. In retrospect, it is clear that investors in these oil companies would have been better served if managers had spent less on new projects and takeovers and more on dividends. That way the investors themselves could have used the dividends to invest in metals companies, or to go into something else instead.

Dividend yields

It is very important for the investor to look at the actual cash pay-out that he or she is getting from the share. As we've seen, this pay-out is the dividend, the most direct source of value in a share. The dividend per share is given in the accounts. In the case of Plessey in 1987–8 it was 6.659 pence per share. (This is the net dividend: tax at the basic rate of income tax has been prepaid by the company.) As we'll see in Chapter 6, it's easy to check the dividend level in the newspaper.

As is the case with the other indicators, we need to compare the dividend from a share with the price of that share if we are trying to assess whether that share is a good buy. The ratio of the annual dividend from a share to the price of that share is known as the dividend yield. It is normally given as a percentage, on a 'gross' (pre-tax) basis.

For example, on 9 September 1988 the price of Plessey shares was 145.5 pence each. The most recent 12 months' net (after-tax) dividend was the 6.659 pence mentioned above. As the basic rate of tax was 25%, this was equal to a gross dividend of 6.659 ÷ 0.75 = 8.88 pence per share. So the dividend yield on Plessey shares was 8.88 ÷ 145.5 = 6.1%. This number is also directly available in the shares pages of newspapers.

Relative returns

Dividend yields can be readily compared across companies in the same industry, between companies in different industries, and with returns expected from other investments. We can compare a 5% dividend yield from a share with, say, a 10% rate of interest on a building society account or a gilt (there's more about both of these in Chapter 3).

If everything else was equal, a high dividend yield would be better than a low one – the investor would be getting a greater cash return on his or her money. As is the case of the other indicators of value, though, everything else isn't always equal. While the company's managers set the dividend level, the price of the shares – the other factor in determining the dividend yield – is set in the market. The yield will be high when the market expects that dividends will be cut; and so it has lowered the price of the shares. This will also be the case if the market expects the dividends not to grow very fast in the future. Often the market will be right.

At the time of writing, shares in high street banks offer relatively high dividend yields. The dividend yields are high because the share prices have been lowered in relation to the current dividend. The market expects the high street banks to encounter such heavy competition in the near future that their profits, and their dividends, will show very little growth.

Dividend yields on shares are usually lower than yields on fixed-income investments. The reason that investors accept a lower yield from shares is that, although future dividend payouts are not certain, the best guess is usually that they will grow over time. Fixed-income returns on the other hand are just that – fixed. An investment of £10 000 in gilts (UK government bonds) at an annual yield of 10% returns interest income of £1000 per year. That £1000 per annum is constant. If instead you own 6873 of the Plessey shares in our example (price 145.5 pence each, gross dividend 8.88 pence), your total investment of £10 000 will return dividends of £610 per year – but you can hope that both the dividends and the capital value of the shares will grow.

Before the 1950s dividend yields were usually higher than yields on fixed-income investments. The same logic was operating, but investors were more concerned about the relative riskiness of shares. Shares haven't got any less risky since then: what's happened is that investors have realised that a return that is fixed in money terms can shrink severely in real buying power because of inflation. Company dividends, on the other hand, offer some protection from inflation, as good shares' dividends will rise. There's more about the impact of inflation on fixed-income investments in Chapter 3.

Company accounts – a summary

The table below is a very simple picture of the way a typical company works, expressed in 'accounting' terms.

Net assets (start of year) + New Investment − Depreciation	=	Net assets (end of year)
Sales − Costs	=	Cash flow
Cash flow − Depreciation	=	Profits after tax (Earnings)
Earnings − Retained Earnings	=	Dividends

Back to the search for value ·

The indicators above, and the raw figures they are taken from, offer the investor ways of determining the true value of a share. In fact the raw data drawn from a company's accounts should be scoured for clues as to the fair value of a company's shares. Comparing this data with the actual share price can help you determine whether or not the share is a good buy.

It is only logical that one such indicator of fair value should be the actual current dividend level. We use the current level of dividends as a guide to what we can reasonably expect will be sustained in the future. This ties in with what we know about managers' behaviour – they are usually reluctant to cut a dividend level once it has been established. So today's dividend level is

make money make money

not a bad indicator of the level which managers think can be sustained in future years. In fact the dividend level is one of the simplest and most important indicators of value. But dedicated hunters for value, and bargains, should also take the other indicators very seriously.

The search for value – why bother?

It's only fair to remember that some intelligent people think that searching for value at all is a waste of time. Recall the Efficient Markets Theory (EMT), which we met in Chapter 4. The EMT says that, because the prices of different shares adjust very fast to reflect all the information (including measures of value) which has an effect on those prices, there is nothing for you to gain by further study of indicators of value. There is no way for you to use today's information to predict tomorrow's price gains or losses. So people who use indicators of value carefully to choose the shares in which they invest will on average do no better than those who use a dartboard.

The EMT is a serious theory. It is intellectually attractive – it is reassuring to non-expert or lazy investors and also implies that most of the activities of share market 'pundits' are a waste of time; there is also some evidence to support it. In particular, there is no evidence at all that simply looking at charts of the recent moves in a share price will help at all in predicting what a share will do next.

I used to believe in the EMT. I now believe that the shares market is highly but not completely efficient: therefore it doesn't always get it completely right. Markets are prone to bouts of optimism or pessimism, which will pull prices away up or down from their 'fair' level. The best way to make money out of these emotional spasms is to buy those shares which look cheap relative to 'objective' criteria: this is the best clue as to which ones are undervalued by the market and will recover.

The ideal indicator

It should be clear from what's been said that none of the indicators of value is perfect. As you might imagine, there have been many attempts to find the one that works best in practice. It may also come as no surprise that no one indicator is a clear winner.

Here are some brief examples of how indicators have been used by professional investors to some effect:

1   The successful corporate raiders of recent years have tended to use a mixture of the 'net asset' and 'cash flow' approaches: the basic idea is either that the raider can sell off the assets to someone else, or that the cash flow from them can be used to pay off the loans taken out to buy the company.

2   Studies by stockbroking firms confirm that buying shares with a low ratio of asset value to price (the net asset approach) would have been a profitable strategy in the UK in the mid-1980s.

3   For many years the *Investors' Chronicle* has regularly created portfolios of shares with high dividend yields, which have usually outperformed the market in later periods.

4   A Cambridge college which runs a highly successful portfolio (reported on from time to time by an 'Academic Investor') uses much the same strategy. It buys the high-yielding shares of established companies which are out of favour with the market ('fallen angels') and waits until they recover.

5   A major study of the performance of shares in the US market between 1966 and 1984 (reported in Ibbotson and Brinson, *Investment Markets*, McGraw-Hill, 1987) shows that the net asset, P/E and dividend yield indicators all worked to some extent.

6   The investment bank Morgan Stanley studied the effectiveness of the net asset, cash flow, P/E and dividend yield indicators in each of the world's main share markets in the 1980s. In the UK market all of these indicators had some usefulness; the net asset approach did best overall.

No one indicator gives a completely reliable guide as to where value can be found. So one sensible approach is to attempt to make use of all of them. In all cases, the share we want is one with a low price relative to the indicator of value. So, for a given share price we want high net asset value, high sales, high cash flow, high earnings, and a high dividend level.

*V*alue versus 'Growth' ·

The general value-based approach is the investment strategy which has made investors like Sir John Templeton and Warren Buffett extremely wealthy men. (Templeton's investment approach is described opposite; there is a good description of Buffett's methods of investment in a book by John Train called *The Midas Touch*.) The 'value' investment strategy leads investors to seek out established companies which have fallen on slightly hard times, or which have merits which the market does not see for some other reason. The strategy implies that the real qualities of a company, which can be inferred from the financial facts about it, sometimes are not fully reflected in the current share price.

Unfortunately, tracking down undervalued shares is not very exciting. It's only fair to say that you are unlikely to find the 'next IBM' through this route: you're much more likely to run into the old IBM when it's having a bad year. Undervalued established companies are not 'sexy'. For this reason, much media attention is focused instead on 'growth' companies. These are companies with new products, or ideas for new products, with potential markets which may be limitless. Growth companies come with a story which can inspire investors. In the late 1980s electronics and biotechnology companies are often good examples.

Going for growth

In growth companies potential is paramount: there is as yet no established value there. Successful investing in growth companies requires much more skill and effort than following the value approach. The investor has to make an accurate assessment of where the company might be in 20 years' time, and of what it might then be worth. There is nothing firm today to go on: often the company exists only in the founders' imagination. Great fortunes can be made by backing such companies at the right time; in other circumstances the investor can lose all or almost all the money put in. The methods for selecting winners are outside the scope of this book. The individual investor, without either the resources or the time to devote to choosing amongst growth companies, is better advised to look for established value.

What such a 'value investor' is doing, essentially, is ironing out irregularities in the market system. The value is there; what is not fully there is the market's appreciation of that value. The investor who searches for value will buy the shares and hope that other people will eventually detect this value too. It is a surer, and safer, way of making moderate amounts of money in the stock-market. But it is unlikely to create huge fortunes in short order.

The Templeton Touch

Sir John Templeton is one of the most successful investors in international shares markets. Indeed, it could be said that he pioneered investment in non-US shares for Americans. The Templeton Growth Fund has one of the best and most consistent records of any international unit trust.

Two major factors condition Templeton's whole approach to life. The first is a concern with spiritual development, 'openness to God', which he believes is integral to his investment success. The second is the 'retreat principle' – Templeton lives and works in the Bahamas, far away from the world's main financial centres. This gives him time and space to think, without being disturbed by other people. His authorised biography, *The Templeton Touch* by William Proctor, lists his investment principles. Some of the most important are:

1   Buy bargains – shares which are selling for less than their true value. This is most likely if you buy shares that other investors aren't keen on, or are selling.

2   Diversify – across companies, industries and countries. The good sense of splitting portfolios across different countries is now well understood in sophisticated investment institutions. But in America at least, Templeton was a pioneer.

3   Be aware of social and political trends. Templeton is highly suspicious of any form of socialism. He also believes that investors should be very wary of inflation.

4   Be flexible in what you buy. No one type of investment is always best. Don't fall into the trap of buying yesterday's winner just because it did well yesterday!

5   Be patient – wait for your investment strategies to work out. Templeton holds shares for many years on average. He only sells shares when he has a better investment with which to replace them. This strategy has the benefit of holding down dealing costs.

6   Do extensive research. Templeton is particularly keen on looking at key numerical information (for example, prospective P/E ratios) on the companies he's interested in, and comparing one with another.

7   Simplicity – remain focused on the basic principles of successful investment. Don't let details cloud your vision.

It's interesting how close some of these principles are to the 'iron laws' of investment set out in Chapter 1 – hunt for value, diversify, don't over-trade.

Privatisations ·

The extensive privatisation programme of the Conservative governments since 1979 has probably done more to encourage individual share ownership in Britain than any other factor. There are two main reasons: the aggressive marketing of the shares of most of the enterprises being privatised; and the fact that the shares were typically underpriced. In most cases they began trading at prices well above those at which they were offered: this meant instant profits for those who managed to buy some of them. This both encouraged participation in each issue at the time, where investors had some idea that the shares would be cheap, and built momentum for successive issues. It also helped persuade inexperienced investors that buying shares was a sure-fire way to fortune.

At the time of writing, the prospects for significant further privatisations appear good. Should you get involved? No universal answer can be given. You'll have to examine the circumstances in each case. In general, future privatisation issues are likely to be useful additions to a share portfolio. Some of the enterprises scheduled for eventual sale are large and represent 'core' parts of the economy (ironically, it was because some were part of what were described as 'the commanding heights' of the economy that they were originally nationalised). As a result, shares in these businesses will be an important part of the whole shares market. So the owner of a diversified portfolio may well want to have something invested in them.

On balance, it is quite likely that the shares offered in many privatisations will continue to be underpriced. Privatisations are likely to continue to be used to spread share ownership rather than to get the best possible prices for the assets. One factor to watch out for is the method of sale. Fixed-price share sales are more likely to provide instant profits than 'tender offers'. In a tender, investors submit their own different offers and the final price set for the shares is the one that balances supply with demand, i.e. the one at which all the shares just get taken up. So prices set in tenders are not likely to undervalue the share on offer.

You should try to find out what the fair price would be in any fixed-price sale. This can change as market conditions change, so leave making any decision to the last moment. This lesson was learnt painfully by those who got involved in the sale of BP shares in late 1987. The sale price was set before share prices crashed, and what had originally been an attractive offer price became very expensive. Follow the financial pages of newspapers closely just before the final due date for applications for any privatisation issue. City experts are usually quite good at estimating the 'fair' price of a new issue relative to other shares, and newspapers will be quick to tell you if the actual price seems to be below this level!

*W*hen to sell ·

Sooner or later, you will want to realise your investments in shares, or to sell one share to buy another. We've seen that shares aren't a suitable parking place for money which you're likely to need in a hurry. Make your sales later if you can! If you're switching one share into another, have a very good reason for doing so – for example, that everyone else has finally recognised the underlying value of a share which you bought when it was cheap, so that it is now at a much higher price!

The reason for saying this is that trading in shares is very expensive. When you buy and sell, it may or may not be a good decision for you; the only certainty is that it's very good news for your stockbroker. The section at the start of this chapter emphasised the role of minimum dealing charges in raising the cost of buying or selling shares. There are other costs, too, although they do not vary with the size of the trade. The buyer of shares pays Stamp Duty of 0.5% of the value of a transaction. Neither the buyer nor the seller gets the mid-market price either: both suffer from the 'touch' or spread between best buying and selling prices which keeps market-makers in champagne.

*S*ummary ·

To sum up, there are three main steps to successful investment in individual shares:

1   You should try to diversify your holdings – not all your investments will work out. You'll have to decide what level of diversification you can afford, though. Dealing charges can dramatically reduce the return to you from even the best-chosen small investments in shares.

2   Dealing charges, and the other costs of buying and selling shares, also mean that you should avoid overtrading. You should have good reasons for selling one share and buying another.

3   The key step in choosing which shares to invest in is to hunt for value. In general, the most successful investors in shares do not chase the latest trend. Instead they try to buy what is unfashionable, and which for that very reason offers a price which is low in relation to its underlying worth.

c h a p t e r · 6

Reading · the · financial · pages ·

This chapter is about how to read the financial pages of newspapers, particularly about how to read the shares pages. The examples are taken from the *Financial Times*.

The *FT* is not the only newspaper which offers this kind of service; most major newspapers now feature shares or 'City' pages of some kind. At the time of writing, coverage is usually most thorough in *The Times*, the *Independent*, the *Guardian* and the *Daily Telegraph* on weekdays; and in the *Sunday Times*, the *Observer* and the *Sunday Telegraph* on Sundays. However, the *FT* is the premier newspaper for City news in the United Kingdom. Its equivalent in the United States is the *Wall Street Journal*. All serious investors will, sooner or later, probably find themselves turning to the *FT* as a source of information.

The *FT* London Stock Exchange page ·

The first thing to get from the financial pages of the newspaper is a picture of what the share market as a whole is doing right now. What we seek is an impression of overall market performance, not simply the movement of any individual share.

Let's turn straight to the London Stock Exchange page of the *FT*. The summary of London Stock Exchange behaviour in the previous trading session is designed to be read simply, and to be informative to the lay reader.

Let's quote a typical opening sentence.

The round of half-point increases in UK base rates found a favourable reception yesterday in London securities markets, which had feared that the Bank of England might push rates by a full point. The City was hopeful that the half-point rise will help to restrain domestic inflation and stabilise the pound.

The report is trying to identify the key influences on the market – the half-point increases in base rates, in our example – and trying to assess their impact. In this case higher interest rates did not produce a negative effect because an even larger increase had been feared.

As it happens, this is an example of a key aspect of share-market behaviour. The share market tries to anticipate what is likely to happen, as well as react to what has already happened. Fears of a full 1% rise in interest rates had already been 'built into' share prices. Financial writers often use the term 'discounted' for a price movement which anticipates a change in market conditions like this. Higher interest rates are generally bad for share prices. In this case, the 'news' as far as the market was concerned was that interest rates had risen by less than had been expected.

Now let's look at the detailed effect. Further on in the report we read that

both bonds and equities bounced higher as market-makers, caught out by the sudden turn in the mood, hurried to buy stock. The about turn in equities took the FT-SE index from an early fall of 13 to a final gain of 15 points ... At the close, the FT-SE 100 index was 15.4 points up, at 1856.9. SEAQ volume of 396.7 million shares (390.7 million on Monday) indicated a brisk but not heavy day's business.

What does all this mean? The first thing to note is the explanation of how prices rose. 'Market-makers', professionals who buy and sell shares for a living, found themselves short of 'stock'. Like a car dealer, a market-maker who finds himself running short of supplies puts in an order for more. In the case of cars, the order eventually reaches a manufacturer who is usually happy to supply more at current prices. This isn't the case with shares. There isn't new 'production' to be had. So instead of buying from a manufacturer of shares, the market-maker has to buy from existing owners. He can normally do this only by offering higher prices. By raising prices, he tempts existing holders of shares to sell them and provide him with his inventory. In effect, enthusiastic buyers prise shares away from existing holders by offering them higher prices. The market-maker makes this possible.

The FT–SE Index ·

A share 'index' provides an easy way to summarise the movements of the whole shares market. The FT–SE index (often known as 'Footsie', as in 'playing footsie') is now the most commonly used simple indicator of UK share-market performance. It shows the price level, on a weighted average basis, of the shares of the 100 most valuable British companies which are quoted on the UK Stock Exchange. (There are equivalent indices in other share markets, for example, the Dow Jones and Standard and Poor's indices in the US, and the Nikkei index in Japan.)

Each company has a weight in the index proportional to its total market value. That means that the shares of the most valuable companies, like British Telecom or BP, have a much larger weight than the less valuable companies at the bottom of the top 100 list. The 100 companies in the FT–SE index at the time of writing are shown in the table alongside. As you can see, they include most of the great names of British industry, often known as 'blue chips' (blue chips are the most valuable ones in the casino!). While there are over 2000 companies' shares traded on the Stock Exchange in Britain, the 100 largest are sufficiently important that their use in this index ensures that it gives a good picture of overall market behaviour. For purposes of simple analysis, the FT–SE 100 is the market. Its shares are also the only ones that I recommend that you get involved in, if you're not an expert investor.

Base dates

Each index like the FT–SE 100 has both a base date and a base value. The FT–SE index started with a base value of 1000 at the end of 1983. That means that the level on the day in our example, 1856.9, shows that between the end of 1983 and the date in question (28 June 1988) those 100 shares' prices had risen on average by some 86%. Had prices trebled over the period the index would stand at 3000; on the other hand, had they fallen by 50% the index would stand at 500.

FT-SE 100 SHARES

Allied-Lyons	Cable & Wireless	Land Securities	Rothmans
Amstrad	Cadbury	Lasmo	Royal Bank of Scotland
Argyll	Coats Viyella	Legal & General	Royal Insurance
Asda	Commercial Union	Lloyds	RTZ
Associated British Foods	Consolidated Gold Fields	Lonrho	Sainsbury
BAA	Cookson	Lucas	Scottish & Newcastle
Barclays	Courtaulds	Marks & Spencer	Sears
Bass	English China Clay	Maxwell Communications	Shell
BAT	Enterprise Oil	MEPC	Smith & Nephew
Beecham	Fisons	Midland	Standard Chartered
BET	Gateway	National Westminster	STC
Blue Circle	GEC	P & O	Storehouse
BOC	General Accident	Pearson	Sun Alliance
BOOTS	Glaxo	Pilkington	Tarmac
BP	Granada	Plessey	Tesco
BPB	Grand Metropolitan	Prudential	Thorn EMI
British Aerospace	GRE	Racal	Trafalgar House
British Airways	Guiness	Rank	Trusthouse Forte
British & Commonwealth	GUS	Reckitt & Colman	TSB
British Gas	Hammerson	Redland	Ultramar
British Steel	Hanson	Reed	Unilever
British Telecom	Hawker Siddeley	Reuters	United Biscuits
BTR	Hillsdown	RHM	Wellcome
Burmah	ICI	RMC	Whitbread
Burton	Ladbroke	Rolls-Royce	Woolworth

The MMMM two-share index

The method of working out the index can be seen using a simple example. Let's create the 'Make Money Make Money 2-share index'. We decide to include only British Telecom and ICI in our index. We also decide that our index will start at 1000. On the next day, the price of British Telecom rises from 250 pence to 260 pence per share, while that of ICI falls from 1000 pence to 980 pence. What should our index do?

	Old	New	Change	%	Weight	Contribution
British Telecom	250	260	+10	+4.0	60	+2.4
ICI	1000	980	−20	−2.0	40	−0.8
Index					100	+1.6

An index can be calculated in a number of different ways. In this case it's done in the same way as the FT–SE index. First work out the percentage change in the price of each share. Then multiply each percentage change for each share by the weight of that share in the index. Different shares have different weights which reflect their importance in the market. In the FT–SE index the weights are proportional to the value of each company. In any index the weights must sum to 100%, and in our example BT has a 60% weight and ICI a 40% weight. So for British Telecom a percentage change of 4% moves the index by 4% × 60% = 2.4%: this is shown in the table as British Telecom's contribution to the index. We then add up the contributions to the index to get the percentage change in the index. In our example this is +1.6%. So the new value of our index should be 1000 + 1.6% = 1016.

The FT–SE index is increasingly quoted as the main indicator of UK share-market behaviour. However, you should be aware of one other index and one other family of indices which are often quoted. To make matters doubly confusing both include the letters FT in their name. That just goes to underline the *Financial Times*' primacy as the main newspaper reporting City news in the United Kingdom.

The FT 30-share industrial average

As the name implies, the FT 30-share industrial average measures moves in 30 industrial shares. It's the 'Ordinary' index recorded in the table at the top of the London Stock Exchange page in the *FT*. The 30-share index has been around for a long time – since the middle of 1935, in fact. On the day when FT–SE was 1856.9, the 30-share index stood at 1473.9. In this case it doesn't mean a 47% rise from the starting value. In fact, the 30-share index started back in 1935 at a value of 100; over the 53 years between 1935 and our example it rose by a factor of almost 15. But it's gradually falling out of use because it contains too small and unrepresentative a sample of shares.

Much of the London Stock Exchange page focuses on why individual companies have had sharp share price movements, and on other economic developments relevant to the market. This can be of great interest if you're interested in shares in companies which are featured. However, there's also more to learn from indices. Turn to the FT-Actuaries Indices page (you will find an example overleaf).

This market statistics page contains a huge amount of information: about the shares market as a whole, about different sectors of the market, and about bonds in the Fixed Interest section (bonds are discussed in Chapter 3).

All in the family

The rest of the shares section is given over to the more detailed FT-Actuaries indices – a 'family' of indices. These focus on companies in different sectors of the economy – in Building Materials, or Chemicals, for example. All the sectors taken together add up to the All-Share index. This is a misnomer: although it covers many more companies than the FT–SE (over 700 in our example) and all major companies, there are still many smaller companies which are not included.

FT-ACTUARIES SHARE INDICES

These Indices are the joint compilation of the Financial Times, the Institute of Actuaries and the Faculty of Actuaries

EQUITY GROUPS & SUB-SECTIONS Figures in parentheses show number of stocks per section	Index No.	Day's Change %	Est. Earnings Yield% (Max.)	Gross Div. Yield% (Act at (25%))	Est. P/E Ratio (Net)	xd adj. 1989 to date	Fri Jan 20 Index No.	Thu Jan 19 Index No.	Wed Jan 18 Index No.	Year ago (approx) Index No.
1 CAPITAL GOODS (208)	849.31	+0.5	11.03	4.20	11.11	0.32	844.98	838.16	829.95	741.25
2 Building Materials (28)	1053.38	+1.3	12.10	4.32	10.17	0.00	1040.26	1034.80	1024.99	974.64
3 Contracting, Construction (39)	1597.70	+0.3	12.40	3.82	10.51	0.00	1593.00	1581.73	1568.88	1452.07
4 Electricals (10)	2469.42	+0.8	8.76	4.57	13.76	0.00	2448.75	2428.42	2400.59	2035.06
5 Electronics (30)	1932.97	-1.0	9.70	3.38	13.34	0.00	1951.61	1929.12	1906.63	1520.81
6 Mechanical Engineering (55)	448.24	+1.1	10.62	4.18	11.46	0.03	443.57	440.79	436.69	387.97
8 Metals and Metal Forming (7)	487.65	+0.7	15.74	6.04	7.18	0.00	484.14	478.41	475.08	441.03
9 Motors (17)	281.12	+1.5	11.72	4.71	9.91	0.00	276.85	275.45	271.41	272.96
10 Other Industrial Materials (22)	1423.88	+0.7	9.67	4.42	12.27	3.28	1414.57	1402.00	1391.32	1256.24
21 CONSUMER GROUP (187)	1095.49	+0.4	9.48	3.83	13.21	0.67	1090.76	1086.36	1077.66	1035.41
22 Brewers and Distillers (22)	1197.16	+0.6	10.64	3.72	11.74	0.00	1189.59	1186.84	1182.43	981.34
25 Food Manufacturing (21)	990.84	+0.3	9.27	3.88	13.52	1.34	988.20	978.89	974.58	855.06
26 Food Retailing (15)	1938.03	-0.6	9.36	3.62	14.06	4.84	1950.63	1924.87	1918.37	2077.77
27 Health and Household (13)	1943.23	+0.5	6.90	2.79	16.60	0.20	1933.59	1926.89	1893.50	1769.50
29 Leisure (32)	1441.70	+0.9	8.38	3.61	15.10	0.00	1428.39	1431.87	1425.18	1178.43
31 Packaging & Paper (17)	568.14	+0.2	9.82	4.03	12.67	0.26	566.92	562.38	553.16	493.09
32 Publishing & Printing (18)	3462.79	+0.6	9.07	4.54	13.80	2.12	3441.48	3437.80	3390.14	3405.12
34 Stores (34)	727.86	+0.8	11.63	4.73	11.31	0.29	721.86	722.13	718.68	840.48
35 Textiles (15)	499.39	-0.4	13.85	5.67	8.65	0.00	501.21	498.43	491.61	589.71
40 OTHER GROUPS (92)	959.33	+0.8	10.72	4.48	11.44	0.07	956.22	958.45	949.65	859.44
41 Agencies (18)	1165.63	+1.1	8.24	2.53	15.31	0.00	1152.63	1137.63	1115.84	1090.12
42 Chemicals (22)	1094.77	+0.1	11.71	4.82	10.29	0.23	1093.69	1090.31	1081.76	1055.95
43 Conglomerates (12)	1336.77	+1.0	10.05	5.36	11.69	0.00	1323.23	1318.29	1298.55	1157.92
45 Shipping and Transport (12)	2022.91	+0.8	9.83	4.12	13.30	0.00	2007.67	2011.26	1988.68	1827.91
47 Telephone Networks (2)	1044.03	-0.3	11.25	4.50	11.56	0.00	1047.17	1060.20	1062.75	902.17
48 Miscellaneous (26)	1294.66	+0.3	11.01	4.23	10.33	0.27	1290.43	1295.15	1270.30	1141.77
49 INDUSTRIAL GROUP (487)	1011.02	+0.4	10.25	4.11	12.06	0.40	1006.72	1003.26	994.40	921.60
51 Oil & Gas (13)	1871.35	+0.2	9.86	5.93	12.98	0.00	1866.70	1840.97	1812.45	1750.50
59 500 SHARE INDEX (500)	1084.03	+0.4	10.20	4.37	12.18	0.37	1079.69	1074.42	1063.94	991.87
61 FINANCIAL GROUP (126)	714.22	+0.6	–	4.99	–	0.15	709.83	711.46	706.05	657.09
62 Banks (8)	708.90	+0.6	20.22	6.18	6.63	0.00	704.92	706.01	705.19	669.78
65 Insurance (Life) (8)	1037.07	+1.9	–	5.20	–	0.00	1017.76	1013.79	981.83	973.19
66 Insurance (Composite) (7)	560.99	+0.6	–	5.57	–	0.00	557.49	559.22	548.82	504.22
67 Insurance (Brokers) (7)	973.10	-0.2	9.00	6.68	13.89	0.00	975.03	962.75	957.82	942.04
68 Merchant Banks (11)	328.26	-0.5	–	4.57	–	0.00	329.95	330.39	329.95	348.64
• 69 Property (53)	1245.24	+0.6	5.82	2.70	21.89	0.05	1238.39	1250.25	1250.82	1012.03
70 Other Financial (32)	364.15	+0.1	9.58	5.52	13.02	0.86	363.62	362.27	359.43	392.79
71 Investment Trusts (76)	998.33	+0.4	–	3.06	–	0.51	993.96	993.71	982.37	838.72
81 Mining Finance (2)	610.64	-0.4	10.01	3.42	11.13	0.00	613.18	613.03	603.00	422.57
91 Overseas Traders (8)	1320.99	+0.2	8.87	4.79	13.07	0.00	1318.10	1308.45	1295.61	1014.01
99 ALL-SHARE INDEX (712)	993.14	+0.4	–	4.41	–	0.31	988.99	985.45	976.01	901.57

	Index No.	Day's Change	Day's High (a)	Day's Low (b)	Jan 20	Jan 19	Jan 18	Jan 17	Jan 16	Year ago
FT-SE 100 SHARE INDEX‡	1924.7	+7.2	1938.6	1917.5	1917.5	1910.8	1892.1	1867.7	1871.8	1762.2

Going left to right across the indices

The information given for each sector is fairly straightforward. The index value is given in the first column after the name, and the second column shows the percentage change from the previous day.

Earnings yield

Next comes the earnings yield – this is the total earnings (profits) over the last year of all the companies in the index for that sector, expressed as a percentage of the sector's market value. For example, if the profits of all 'Oil and Gas' companies in the index (BP, Shell and others) add up to £5 billion, and the market values of these companies add up to £40 billion, the earnings yield will be $100 \times 5 \div 40 = 12.5\%$.

It's important to remember that this is not the 'profitability' of the industry so much as the profitability that the shares market requires the industry to have! If investors were very keen on oil companies, the total value of the sector might rise from £40 billion to £100 billion. If the earnings were still £5 billion, the earnings yield would then be only 5%. Alternatively, the value of the sector could fall to £20 billion if investors were more gloomy, and the earnings yield would then be 25%!

This is broadly what's happened to bank shares in our example. At this time, many investors did not believe that banks' profits were reliable or sustainable. As a result, bank shares are low relative to earnings. In our example the earnings yield is over 20% – but this is a measure of investors' pessimism, not of banks' prosperity.

Dividend yield

The next column shows the gross (i.e. pre-tax) dividend yield, which is the total dividends which the companies in the sector have actually paid out to their shareholders in the last year as a percentage of the total value of the sector. Again this is the dividend payout 'required' by investors. We saw in the section on 'value' (page 102) that in theory the value of a share – or a sector – is the expected value of all future dividends from it, adjusted for risk and the delay in getting the money.

The highest dividend yields amongst the major sectors are those for banks and oil companies. The lowest, where investors have more confidence in the growth and stability of future dividends, are in agencies (for example, in advertising and temporary employment) and 'health and household' companies (for example, drug companies). The market believes that for these sectors even better times are just around the corner.

Price/Earnings

The next column shows the sector's price/earnings (P/E) ratio. The P/E ratio, as discussed on page 108, is one of the most widely used indicators of relative value in the shares market. As its name implies, P/E for an individual share is the share price divided by earnings (profits) per share. For a sector, it's the total market value of the sector divided by total sector earnings. Again this is a measure of investors' confidence in a particular industry. A high P/E means that investors have confidence that profits will grow strongly in future. They're willing to pay many pounds now to get hold of shares which last year generated one pound's worth of earnings.

The XD adjustment

The next column shows what's called the XD adjustment. That shows you what dividends you would have been entitled to from holding all the shares in the sector since the start of the year. So at the end of the year you can add the XD adjustment to the change in the index level, to measure the total return from the sector. The XD total shows the dividend return, while the change in the index shows the capital gain or loss.

The rest of the columns show recent index levels, as well as the levels a year ago. When you compare current index levels with these numbers, you can get some idea of the way a sector has been moving.

How to use the indices to make money

You can learn a lot from these tables. For example, it is clear that dividends vary across sectors. Yields also differ; we've already examined some reasons why this is so.

In our example, banks yield 6.18% and agencies yield 2.53%. The difference in dividend yield then is 3.65% per year between the sectors. That doesn't necessarily mean that the investor should prefer banks' shares. The reason that the dividend yields differ is that all investors in aggregate (individuals, pension funds, other companies, etc.) have taken the view that the value of shares in agencies will grow faster than the value of shares in banks. This has driven up the share price of agencies, which in turn has lowered their dividend yield. This hidden expectation explains the dividend gap between the sectors. If you don't agree with the market's expectations, then this column offers you a clue about where to start looking for good investments. Go against the trend and you may make money.

Back to the future?

Another way to use the table is to look at the present level of shares against past history. This too can give us a clue as to over- or undervaluation.

An example. For the day we're looking at, the FT-Actuaries All-Share index shows a level 10.2% above its year-ago level. For the stores sector, on the other hand, there has been a fall of 13.4%. You might believe that this relative trend will continue – in which case you'd want to avoid stores shares. On the other hand, you might believe that stores have fallen too far and are due for a relative recovery. Either way, a look at where shares have been before arriving at their present levels can be a useful guide as to where they might be about to go, and valuable for investment decision-making.

Buying the sector?

Looking at different sectors of the shares market is a good way of starting the search for investments. However, it's only the start. Don't adopt a policy of simply buying shares in only one or two sectors. Investing in one or two sectors which you believe are undervalued exposes you to a higher level of risk than if you spread your investments across several sectors. You can't be absolutely sure that your chosen sector will do well.

BP and Shell are different companies; their shares do not perform identically. However, their performances are much more closely related than those of BP and, for example, Hanson Trust. The point is that both BP and Shell are subject to the forces that influence all oil company shares – movements in the oil price, changes in weather, changes in the tax on petrol, etc. As a result, their shares tend to move up and down together. If your portfolio contains just oil company shares it will not be very well diversified – and you'll be running a high level of financial risk.

*I*ndividual shares ·

You usually can't invest in the share market as a whole, or in whole sectors – only in the shares of individual companies. So you need to know what the financial pages can tell you about individual shares. In the *Financial Times* the 'London Share Service' consists of two full pages of closely-set detail about individual companies quoted in the UK market. You can also check the prices of the leading shares quoted in foreign markets: but the analysis of these markets is beyond the scope of this book.

Categories

If you're trying to track down a specific share, you need to know which category it falls into. Normally this is self-evident but there are a few surprises for the non-expert: for example, Reckitt and Colman turns up under 'Industrials (Miscel.)' rather than 'Food, Groceries, etc.'. This is because, as far as the *FT* is concerned, Reckitt and Colman makes significantly more things like shoe polish and brushes than things like mustard.

The order of the shares is alphabetical within each category.

Highs and lows

Let's see what we can learn about just one company: the well-known super-market chain which appears in 'Food, Groceries, etc.' as Sainsbury (J.). The two columns on the left of the company name show the highest and lowest prices recorded for the share in the year so far – in our example, 250 pence and 188 pence per share respectively. So we immediately know that Sainsbury's shares have fluctuated between those limits (the 'trading range') in the year to date. On Mondays, highs and lows are not shown and are replaced by the 'market capitalisation' (total market value) in millions of pounds for the company.

†5.25	1.3	5.4	(16.8)
L2.0	4.1	1.9	13.4
1.8	φ	3.2	φ
u2.4	1.0	3.6	37.0
14.7	2.1	5.7	10.7
hQ9.09%	–	4.9	–
0.7	–	2.5	–
Q13¾%	1.1	5.0	18.0
g1.5	13.9	0.7	14.9
Q28c	–	1.8	–
B–	–	–	–
–	–	–	14.7
LQ2.57c	3.9	1.4	20.6
†2.7	5.5	1.7	14.3
†L2.63	5.0	1.6	17.0
†3.6	4.3	2.4	13.1
M1.0	4.5	3.2	29.0
7.5	3.2	3.2	13.1
†3.0	5.4	2.0	12.7
3.6	3.6	3.5	10.3
Q5¾%	–	7.4	–
vQ20%	2.1	5.7	7.7
8.5	4.1	3.7	8.5
8.5	4.1	4.6	7.0
†7.4	φ	4.2	φ
†2.8	3.7	3.4	10.5
†6.66	2.3	3.7	14.3
♦0.5	8.1	0.3	25.4
1.75	7.0	1.9	10.0
1.0	5.3	1.8	11.1
7.25	–	8.2	–
u1.75	4.3	1.4	23.6
♦5.4	2.5	2.7	19.1
†4.46	3.2	1.8	21.5
7%	27.9	5.2	–
R1.28	4.2	0.7	45.6
g1.5	5.0	2.6	10.6
th2.13	3.6	2.1	17.3
d2.0	2.9	5.1	9.1
3.3	5.3	2.2	13.4
L2.5	2.6	2.8	16.2
F3.5	*2.5	4.9	10.0
0.65	–	1.0	–
†7.0	3.5	3.0	12.6
L4.4	2.8	2.9	16.4
†1.6	3.9	1.9	18.3
♦6.8	2.0	3.6	17.4

2.16	5.9	1.1	19.7
†4.5	5.0	φ	4.5
†d2.2	3.4	3.0	13.0
†Q88%	7.0	0.6	23.2
2.2	φ	5.1	φ
1.5	6.0	1.5	14.7
†1.41	4.7	2.7	10.0
3.38	6.3	1.7	12.5
†5.0	1.5	‡	16.7
Q80%	φ	0.9	φ
L4.75	0.1	9.7	–
L4.75	2.2	4.6	9.6
0.65	–	0.9	–
Q11%	φ	5.7	φ
†22.0	2.3	4.1	13.2
7%	36.8	5.3	–
5.8	5.9	2.1	11.0
Q14%	3.1	0.7	49.0
4.0	φ	1.8	φ
L2.5	4.2	4.9	5.9
†7.0	3.7	2.1	17.4
Q49.19%	2.9	2.9	12.6
9.07	2.0	5.1	12.0
7.3	φ	5.3	φ
†4.5	5.8	2.4	9.6

Food (central listings)

High	Low	Stock	Price	+/–	Div				52wk Hi	52wk Lo
212	143½	Gateway Corp 5p...α	179	....	†8.0	1.7	6.3	11.8	45	28
298	219	Geest 5p............β	264	+3	†4.0	3.1	2.0	20.8	186	151
95	33	✵Global Grp. 10p. γ	43	+2	1.75	2.1	5.4	10.3	26	10½
135	70	G'dman Fldr Watt $Ao 5.	100	+1	GQ9.75c	3.2	4.7	8.1	°290½	228
437	370	Greggs 20p......... γ	402	....	†7.5	3.2	2.5	16.7	146	68
260	208	Hazlewood 10p.... β	245	+9	†2.6	5.1	1.4	17.1	195	150
307	226	Hillsdown Hldgs 10p α	276	+5½	†4.75	4.2	2.3	11.8	146	100
111	40	✵Hughes Food 5p.. β	46	....	1.5	3.2	4.3	9.0	240	170
°198	135	Hunter Saphir..... β	157	–1	4.05	2.7	3.4	13.9	125	38
373	280	Iceland Frozen 10p.. β	324	+7	M5.25	4.0	2.2	17.1	99	56
27¾	18	✵Israel (Jack L.) 4p .β	20½	....	†0.6	1.9	3.9	17.7	£14¾	797
313	203	Jacob (W.&R.)....γ	313	....	†Q33.7%	3.0	2.3	15.5	80	43
414	300	Kwik Save 10p.... β	414	+13	7.8	3.0	2.5	16.7	156	128
°117	62	Lees (John J) 10p.. γ	108	....	g†1.88	3.3	2.3	17.8	249	167
269	184½	Low (Wm.) 20p.... β	269	....	h5.67	3.0	2.8	15.0	235	182
103	60	✵M6 Cash & Carry γ	95	+9	†3.8	1.7	5.3	13.2	1215	887
98	68½	Matthews (B)........β	84	–1	†1.75	3.6	2.8	13.2	295	267
368	203	Meat Trade Sup... γ	368	....	3.7	0.7	1.3	–	127	43½
269	222½	Morris' n(W.) 10p .β	262	....	†2.0	8.1	1.0	16.1	302	218
104	87	Do. 5¼pc Cm Rd Cv Pf . γ	94	–1	5.25	–	7.4	–	376	284
265	230	Nichols (Vimto)... γ	235	....	†7.75	2.5	4.4	12.3	203	108
295	195	Norish............... γ	210	+5	Q62.6%	2.6	6.7	8.3	272	203
69½	45	Normans Group 10p .β	65½	....	†h1.96	2.3	4.0	11.7	228	193
314	243	Northern Foods.... α	310	+½	†10.0	2.5	4.3	11.8	220	135
116	71	✵Northbr'n Fds.5p.. γ	81	+3	2.0	2.3	3.3	13.3	206	142
196	121	Nurdin P'k. 10p... β	195	–1	†4.3	2.9	2.9	15.8	°84	53
247	169	Park Food 10p.... γ	174xd	–2	†5.3	2.5	4.1	13.1	118	104
°93	55	✵Perkins Foods..... γ	91	+1	†g1.8	1.9	2.6	26.1	183	134
104	60	Ptarmigan 12½p . γ	60	....	Z0.25	–	0.6	–	178½	123½
490	303	RHM .... α	394	+½	10.61	2.7	3.6	12.9	£138	£116
°67½	34½	✵Regina Health 2p.. γ						20.7	132	102
250	188	Sainsbury (J.)...... α	237	+2½	†4.2	3.0	2.4	18.4	73	49
175	130	✵Salvesen Christian						14.9	140	95
°442	330	✵Sims Food Grp 5p.. γ	345xa	+8	†g6.9	2.4	2.6	21.0	°66	37
78	38	✵Sutherland Hldgs... γ	78	+2	†1.1	2.1	1.9	30.1	°158	10
244	185	Tate & Lyle......... α	236	–2	7.38	q2.8	4.2	9.7	335	152
121½	100	Do. 7.25p Cv.Rd.Pf .γ	119½	+½	7.25	–	8.1	–	217	113
103	81	Tavener Rut. 20p...	81	....	1.25	4.7	2.1	10.3	53½	19½
172	126½	Tesco 5p............ α	159	+1	†2.85	3.8	2.4	14.5	38	17
140	126	Thorntons 10p..... β	140	....	L2.1	2.3	2.0	19.5	135	78
368½	253	Unigate............ α	368½	+5	†12.65	2.2	4.6	13.2	93	55
331	248	United Biscuits... α	331	+11½	†11.0	2.1	4.4	13.3	272½	204
189	112	Do. Wrrnts. ('89). β	189	+12					331½	220
118	55	Do. Wrrnts. ('91)...	118	+3					190	116
68	43	✵Wardell Robertslr10p γ	63	....	†Q28.7%	2.8	3.8	11.7	388	288
230	187	Watson & Phlp 10p .β	206	+3	9.4	1.6	6.1	13.9	205	180
£24	£16½	Wessanen (Kon) DFl5.	£22½	–½	Q44.8%	2.4	2.8	14.8	250	171
									150	138
									230	123
									148	64
									397	296
									355	171
									80	52

HOTELS AND CATERERS

High	Low	Stock	Price	+/–	Div				52wk Hi	52wk Lo
111	46	✵Aberdeen Stk 5p.. γ	55	....	1.5	2.6	3.6	14.2	77	48
81	48	✵Allied Rests. 5p... γ	53	+2	1.5	3.4	3.8	9.4	48	29
280	188	Friendly Hotels 10p. β	280	+1	nM2.7	6.6	1.3	(18.4)	155	96
		For Grand Met. see Beers, Wines & Spirits							283	170
70	55	✵Harmony Leisure5p γ	69	+1	0.14	4.4	0.3	83.1	29	16
372	128	IoM Enterprises 5p... γ	252	....	Q45%	φ	0.9	φ	260	108
118	95	Jurys Hotel .... γ	118	....	Q23.08%	1.9	4.1	18.3	560	228
514	322	Ladbroke 10p...... α	499	....	†13.89	2.4	3.7	14.7	58	38
47	20	✵Mandarin Oriental Intl..	39½	–½					203	112
174	108	Mt. Charlotte 10p.β	170	–1	†1.9	4.1	1.5	20.1	518	193
38	24	Norfolk Capital 5p.. β	35½	–½	†0.45	2.1	1.7	31.4	122	71
°116	82	Queens Moat 5p.... β	114	+1	g†1.9	3.0	2.2	18.3	135	71
205	166	Do. 7ccCv. Pf. £1... γ	201	+2	7%	x	4.6	–	39	39
°19	15	✵Resort Hotels 10p.. γ	18xd	....	gL0.42	2.7	3.2	16.4	525	393
°60	18	✵Ryan Hotels lr 5p... γ	39	+1	Q44.12%	–	4.7	–	393	242
1175	733	Savoy "A" 10p.....β	838	+3	5.0	5.6	0.8	26.1	450	340
114	81	Stakis 10p...........β	104½	–2½	1.95	φ	2.5	φ	133	96
284	211	Trusthouse Forte...α	278	+4½	8.4	q2.3	4.1	12.4	91	65
									55	40
									40½	31½
									455	280
									455	355
									°309	138
									625	275

INDUSTRIALS (Miscel.)

High	Low	Stock	Price	+/–	Div				52wk Hi	52wk Lo
203	92	AAF Invs. 7½p..... γ	197	–1	†3.75	3.6	2.5	12.7	140	71
324	251	AAH.................β	322	....	†10.22	2.5	4.2	11.4	116	56
									°700	295

Alphas

Next to the name of the company is a Greek letter – in this case, the letter alpha (α). That indicates that Sainsbury is an 'alpha' share – one of the 100 or so largest and most liquid shares in the market. The overlap between alpha stocks and membership of the FT–SE 100 index is very close. The first column to the right of the company name shows us yesterday's price of the share at the close of business. This is 237 pence (almost all prices are quoted in pence per share). The column next to the price shows the change in price from the previous close: in this example, a rise of 2.5 pence.

The *FT* lists all the alpha shares every day, in alphabetical order, in a table called 'Trading Volume in Major Stocks'. As you might expect, this shows the number of shares traded on the previous day as well as the price.

Bid and Offer

In fact, you couldn't have dealt in Sainsbury shares at 237 pence even at the close. The 237 is the average of the 'bid' and 'offer' prices for the share. The bid price is what a market-maker is prepared to pay for the share, i.e. the price your broker can get for you if you're selling it. Somewhat higher is the offer price; this is the price that you'd have to pay to acquire a share.

The not-so-gentle touch

The difference between bid and offer is the way that the market-maker makes his profit. This spread or 'touch' is lowest for alpha shares, where competition and liquidity is highest. (The 'liquidity' of any market means the volume of money ready and willing to buy and sell in that market.) At the time of writing, a typical spread for an alpha share is about 1% of the mid-price. The next class of shares are 'Beta' (β) shares – there are some 500 of these. Here liquidity is good, but not perfect. Spreads tend to be wider – as much as 4% at the time of writing.

Gammas and deltas

'Gamma' (ψ) and 'delta' (δ) shares are those of still-smaller companies and are even less liquid. There are often very few market-makers in these shares, and they don't get much press coverage. At the time of writing, spreads in gammas and deltas are typically 5% or more. This means that the costs of getting in and out of gammas and deltas are much higher than the costs of dealing in alphas. (Remember that the spread is not the only cost of dealing: you also have to pay commission to the broker or other dealing service who makes the trade for you, and Stamp Duty if you are buying.)

Because bid-to-offer spreads are so much wider for small companies' shares, and also because these shares are usually riskier, I recommend that you steer clear of them. A useful rule is that you should only get involved when both of two conditions apply: first, that you can definitely leave your money in for many years (which reduces the dealing-cost and risk problems); and second, that for some reason you personally know a lot about the business in which 'your' small company is involved (which is another way of holding down the risk level).

'Penny shares', so called because of their rock-bottom prices, are always in the gamma or delta categories.

Dividends

Continuing with the Sainsbury example, the next column shows the net dividend that each share has paid out in the last year (in our example, 4.2 pence). This is the actual cash amount that the owner of one share would have received over the last 12 months, with the company having already paid income tax at the basic rate.

We can adjust this net dividend to work out the gross dividend yield (the dividend yield before tax). The gross dividend yield appears in the next-but-one column. At the time of our example the basic rate of income tax is 25%; so the net dividend paid (4.2 pence) is only 75% of the gross dividend. The gross dividend must be $4.2 \div 0.75 = 5.6$ pence per share. The gross dividend yield is this value expressed as a percentage of the share price: $100 \times 5.6 \div 237 = 2.4\%$, which indeed is the value which appears in the relevant column.

Cover

The column between the net dividend and the gross dividend yield shows the 'cover' for the dividend. This is the ratio of the last year's earnings (profits) to dividends: in Sainsbury's case, 3.0. In other words, if Sainsbury had paid out all its profits to shareholders, the dividend would have been three times bigger than it actually was. Instead, two-thirds of the profits were ploughed back into making the company bigger.

When a company's earnings are many times its dividend the dividend is usually secure – but the investor should check that the company is spending the rest of the profits (the retained earnings) wisely. Cover below or just above one usually means that a company expects that earnings will rise, and that they want to retain investors' confidence by paying out high dividends. This may happen with a 'cyclical' company (one whose results are highly sensitive to the general state of the economy) which is going through a bad patch. Here the problem for the investor is in deciding if the bad patch really is temporary: if it's not, the dividend will eventually be cut.

P/E ratio

The last column in the table shows the price-to-earnings (P/E) ratio. In Sainsbury's case the value is 18.4. This P/E is 'historic': this means that it compares the current share price with the last available figure for 12 months of earnings. Most companies publish their earnings every six months (some every three months); so historic earnings figures, as quoted on the shares page, are therefore slightly out of date.

Analysts and commentators often write about 'prospective P/Es'. These compare the current share price with the earnings which they (the analysts) expect the company to achieve this year or next. It's important that you're aware of what type of P/E is being used. Historic and predicted earnings can differ greatly, particularly for fast-growing and cyclical companies. Although analysts put a lot of work into predicting earnings, their forecasts are often wide of the mark.

Using the information

The figures on the shares page are a good way of getting to know something about the financial basics of different companies. You can use them for comparative purposes: how does Sainsbury's yield and P/E compare with ICI's, for example? Unfortunately, there is no easy way to use these figures to make your fortune overnight. As is the case with the figures for different sectors, 'the market' – which is simply the total of everyone involved in it – has its 'reasons' for the different ratings it gives to different shares. Making a fortune depends on knowing whether those reasons are right or wrong. This book can't tell you how: but the section on 'Value' in Chapter 5 tries to suggest a few clues.

*U*nit trusts ·

For those not interested in direct share investment, the financial pages also contain a lot of information on unit trusts. This information differs by type of unit trust. The first section deals with what are called authorised unit trusts.

Authorised trusts

These are trusts authorised by the UK authorities. We recommend that you do not get involved in any unauthorised trusts! The trusts are arranged alphabetically, by name of manager. Under each manager's name are the different unit trusts which that manager offers.

While the names of the trusts offer some clue as to the kinds of securities which they invest in, names are far from an infallible guide. One firm's idea of what should be in a 'high income' trust may be very different from another's. You should always find out as much as you can about the strategy of a trust before investing in it.

Initial charges

The first number shown next to each trust is the initial charge that the managers levy when you buy units in their fund; it's given as a percentage. Suppose the number is 5%. When you first put, say, £1000 into that trust, the managers take £50 for expenses and buy you units to the tune of £950 only. Initial charges are a substantial burden and remove much of the incentive to get involved in unit trusts. Clearly you want to look out for trusts with low initial charges, if possible.

Prices

The next three columns show the cancellation, bid and offer prices of the units themselves. As with individual shares, the bid and offer prices are the prices at which you can sell and buy units respectively. At least, the bid price applies in normal circumstances. If there is heavy selling of units, as occurred in some cases during the crash in late 1987, the managers can decide to buy back units only at the lower 'cancellation' price. The gap between the offer price and the cancellation price is the maximum that the government allows. In that sense the cancellation price offers some protection to investors.

One guide to the current health of a trust is the gap between the cancellation price – the rock-bottom price – and the bid price. A small gap or no gap indicates that there's fairly intensive selling pressure on the unit trust; that in turn may mean that it's not sensible for you to get involved at this stage. In normal circumstances, however, you want to look at the gap between the bid and offer prices. As with individual shares, this is the cost to you of dealing. Clearly, everything else being equal, you want to go for a unit trust where the gap between bid and offer is small.

The next column shows the change in the mid-price (between bid and offer) since the last quotation. Just as with individual shares, this shows whether prices are rising or falling. In general when shares have a good day, the unit trusts which invest in those shares will have a good day as well. The final column in the authorised unit trust section shows the gross yield on the units. This is precisely akin to the dividend yields shown for individual shares.

Insurance company unit trusts

Insurance company unit trusts are unit trusts run by insurance companies. Their *FT* entries, in a separate section, are slightly less complicated than for normal unit trusts: here we have simply bid and offer prices, the change since the last quotation, and gross yield information where available. This information is also given for off-shore and overseas funds.

Other sources of information

If you go into a unit trust you are really hiring a set of managers for your money. Unfortunately, the basic data on unit trusts in the shares pages do not tell you how good they will be; that's impossible, of course. What you can get from other sources – for example, the monthly magazine *Money Management* – is a better idea of how good they've been in the past relative to other trusts of the same type.

The tables in *Money Management* divide unit trusts into sections (for example, UK Income trusts, which are those which focus on UK shares with relatively high dividend yields) based on simple and clear-cut rules. They also show the performance record of each trust over several time periods – for example, the last five years. So you can use the tables first to focus on trusts in the area you're particularly interested in, and then to see which trusts have the best records in this area. There's no guarantee that the best in the past will go on doing well, of course!

c h a p t e r · 7

*F*utures · *and* · *options* ·

This chapter is about very-high-risk investments; it carries a 'wealth warning' – very-high-risk investments can seriously damage, or completely wipe out, your wealth. You should not get involved in options or futures unless you know exactly what you're doing, and you have the kind of temperament that can stand violent fluctuations in the value of your investment, and you can afford to lose all the money that you put in.

That doesn't mean that the other investment types that we've looked at in earlier chapters are completely risk-free, of course; they're not. Each of the different assets carries its own types of risk; the alert investor is aware of these risks, and takes only those that he or she feels comfortable with. But most of the investments already discussed do not have the potential either to make you a fortune in short order or to wipe you out completely. Futures and options have precisely those features. As a result, they're not for anyone who can't afford to lose all the money that they put into them.

*F*utures ·

A future is a contract to buy something, at a specified price, at some future date. Futures grew out of forward contracts: forward contracts were being traded as far back as Saxon times, when fish merchants used to sell forward fish at Billingsgate in London.

What was (or is) a forward fish? What happens is that you, a keen buyer, agree now that you will pay a specified sum of money for an amount of fish that the fish merchant will deliver to you *at a future date*. He can't deliver it to you now because the catch isn't in yet; you probably don't want the fish now either. But the merchant has a guaranteed sale, and you know that you'll get your fish at the date and price you've specified.

That's a forward contract. It is specific; that is to say, it specifies you as the buyer, the merchant as the seller, and the precise product that's being traded. It's just as if you'd arranged with the merchant to supply you with fish today: the only difference is that the transaction will take place in the future.

What happens if for some reason you decide that you would like to sell your right to buy this fish in the future? You may well have problems in doing so. No one else may want to deal with the merchant you are dealing with at precisely the time you're dealing with him, or for precisely the fish that you've arranged to buy from him. You have a very specific contract, drawn up by you, that may be of limited use or value to anyone else.

Back to the future

The same problem arose with the expansion of agriculture in the Great Plains of North America in the middle part of the nineteenth century. There, too, people wanted to trade goods forward. For example, a rancher shipping cattle from the grazing grounds of Texas up to Chicago wanted to get his price guaranteed before he set out along the trail. A farmer harvesting his wheat might well be unable to transport it to the Great Lakes until after the winter was over, but he too wanted to 'lock in' an acceptable price ahead of delivery.

While these producers could enter into specific forward contracts this involved risk: for example, if the buyer on the other side went bankrupt in the intervening months, the seller would then have to find someone else, possibly at poorer prices. It was more attractive to all involved – particularly as they were dealing in more or less standard commodities (one bushel of wheat is pretty much like another) – to enter into a universally accepted contract.

Futures contracts

The result was the creation of standardised futures contracts, traded on organised exchanges like the Chicago Board of Trade and the Chicago Mercantile Exchange. All the important elements of each contract are defined. For example, there is a standard volume per contract – e.g. 5000 bushels of a certain weight of wheat; this wheat must be of a certain guaranteed quality –

in other words with no more than a certain percentage of moisture in it and free of rust; the wheat is deliverable on a standard date – the last trading day in September, say; and the place of delivery is standardised also – for example, to a grain elevator in one specified street in Chicago.

It isn't always possible for participants in a futures contract to meet these rules precisely, so the Exchanges also build in allowances for variations around the standard conditions. For example, if the farmer wants to deliver his wheat to a different grain elevator he incurs a pre-specified 'penalty' of so many cents per bushel. The key is that the items being traded are sufficiently similar that everyone can agree to live by the rules.

The pits

All those who trade a particular contract gather in their specific 'pit' each day. They buy and sell with each other, either on their own behalf or for others. All deals are reported to the Exchange, which then undertakes to honour each contract. So if you buy a September wheat future and hold it until it matures, the Exchange is responsible for getting the actual wheat to you. Getting the wheat from the trader who sold you the contract is also the Exchange's problem.

Thus there are two important advantages of futures for farmers, merchants, and investors: each contract is identical, with precisely-defined rules that everyone knows about; and 'performance' is guaranteed, no matter what happens to the trader originally on the other side. This means that it is possible to attract lots of money into the business of reducing risk ('hedging' in financial parlance) for producers and users of farm commodities. A contract ('paper wheat') is created every time traders agree a deal amongst themselves. There is no need for it to refer to a specific freight car's-worth of the physical commodity; much more paper wheat can be created and traded than there is actual physical wheat to back it up.

In fact, most contracts don't run to maturity. The owner of a future will often sell it before delivery, thus reducing his net position with the Exchange to zero. However, the prices of the contracts are always tied to the expected actual prices of the wheat – otherwise people would be able to make profits by holding on to their paper positions and actually either delivering or receiving the physical wheat. When a contract finally expires, its value will be equal to that of the physical amount of wheat it represents.

Soya, cattle and live hogs

The first organised futures contracts existed in agricultural products. They're still very important today. In Chicago, for example, there are active futures contracts in soya beans, soya bean oil, soya bean meal, maize, wheat, live cattle, live hogs, and pork bellies. The Chicago contracts reflect the products which are produced in the agricultural hinterland of the Midwest of the United States. In New York, by contrast, globally traded products have futures contracts of their own – cocoa, coffee, sugar, cotton, and orange juice, for example. Futures contracts in agricultural products were rapidly copied from the United States by Britain. In London today there are active futures contracts in cocoa, coffee, sugar, wheat, barley, potatoes, and soya bean meal.

So what is the usefulness of commodity futures contracts to the producer and consumer? Return to the wild Midwest of a century ago. Chicago had become the greatest agricultural market in the world. Railway lines and roads converged on it from all over the Midwest of the United States, allowing farmers to bring their produce to market where it could be processed and then shipped on – either by rail or by ship – to the great consuming centres of the East Coast of the United States and further afield.

However, the transportation of the product from where it was being produced to Chicago was a lengthy business. It took Texan ranchers' large herds of cattle several months to arrive in Chicago, and when they did arrive the rancher might well find that the price for the cattle was either very high (because not many other herds had managed to make the trip successfully) or very low (because large numbers had arrived in Chicago). Ranchers found it impossible to predict whether getting to Chicago would mean bonanza or bust: an entire season's profits could be wiped out if prices were unusually low. On the other hand, if prices were high, it could severely affect the profitability of the operations of the meat-packers who bought the cattle: often they would have already sold on the final product – butchered meat – and would be severely affected if the price they had to pay was unusually high.

This was clearly an unsatisfactory state of affairs. So the Future was born.

What the future holds

The futures contract allowed – and still allows – both sides to 'hedge their bets': to lock in a price ahead of time for as much or as little of the physical trade as they wish. The rancher can sell a 'live cattle' futures contract long before his actual cattle come to market. Then, if the price for his actual cattle is particularly low when they do arrive, he will make an offsetting profit in the futures market. Recall that the price of the cattle futures contract is closely tied to the actual price of the cattle: if actual prices are low, the futures price will be low too. Our rancher can buy back his contract to sell so many cattle at a fixed price in the future for less than he paid for it originally: this both eliminates his obligation to supply the agreed number of cattle at a date in the future and makes him a profit.

The profit on the futures contract offsets the theoretical 'loss' (relative to earlier prices) that the rancher makes on the delivery of actual cattle. He has locked in the price of cattle that applied at the time when he took out the futures contract; from then on he is hedged. He has made a profit, in effect, through selling and then buying back an agreement to deliver a number of theoretical (or 'paper') cattle that never physically existed. This profit is sufficient to offset a price fluctuation on the sale of his actual cattle which could have made him a poor man.

On the other side the meat-packer can buy a futures contract in live cattle. Should the price prove unusually low when they arrive at market, the meat-packer will not benefit: although he will get physical cattle cheaply, he will simultaneously be 'closing out' (selling) his futures contract, receiving much less for it than he originally paid. Thus his chance for exceptional gain has been reduced, but this was the price of removing his downside risk.

The investment opportunity

Where is the opportunity for the investor in all this? Well, we've seen elsewhere in this book that risk normally carries with it return. Ranchers, when they sell cattle futures contracts, are getting risk reduction; they should be prepared to pay something for this service, and indeed they are. On average, the rancher will accept a slightly lower price if he can hedge his risks than he will if he has to bear them all himself.

On the other side of any futures contract, opposite the 'hedger', is the person who is prepared to bear risk. That person, the risk-taker, may be able to get a return by doing so. That is why so many traders without the slightest interest in taking delivery of any cattle or live hogs enter the market. They take risks and, they hope, make a profit.

The price of cattle is extremely important to the income of the rancher. It's not surprising that he's prepared to give up some of his average income in exchange for smaller fluctuations in that income. For the pure investor, on the other hand, live cattle are unlikely to be so important. By bearing some of the risk of fluctuations in the price of cattle, and hopefully getting a return from bearing this risk, the investor may be better off.

*In*vesting in futures ·

All futures investment is based on the premise that you think that the price that you are paying for the contract now is unsustainably low or high. For instance, if you believe that wheat prices will rise, then buying a futures contract to buy wheat now should allow you to sell the contract later at a profit. In normal circumstances you will sell the contract long before delivery would occur; otherwise you will find yourself the proud owner of many thousands of bushels of unwanted wheat, which is inconvenient unless you live in a grain elevator. Conversely, if you expect that wheat prices will fall you would sell a futures contract now, in the expectation of buying it back for less later on.

Why are futures so risky, then? There are two reasons.

Price volatility

The first reason is simply the volatility in the prices of the underlying goods. These can be grains, cattle, other sorts of food commodity, metals – or even exotic financial instruments like futures contracts which deal in a basket of 500 shares. But why are the prices of these things particularly volatile?

We've looked at the background to the volatility in some of the financial assets in earlier chapters. However, the prices of basic foodstuffs and raw materials are also highly volatile. At first sight this may be surprising: you would think that the demand for these basic goods would be fairly stable.

That, in fact, is part of the problem: demand for many commodities is insensitive to variations in price (economists would say that demand is 'price-inelastic'). People will go on buying food, almost whatever the price. They have to; otherwise they starve.

However, supply is not constant. Harvests can fail, because of drought, excessive rain, or plagues of locusts; there can be strikes in mines which supply metals. A host of factors can lead to 'shocks' to supply, which the price mechanism has to cope with. The 1988 drought in the Midwestern states of America, for example, resulted in half their harvest being lost. As a result, futures in wheat, corn and soya beans climbed.

Precisely because demand for commodities like wheat is so stable when prices change, prices will rise a long way when supplies are unusually low. Similarly, prices have to fall a long way to encourage buyers if supply is unusually high. The net result is that, while volumes may not fluctuate very much, the prices in the market go up and down with wide variations.

In fact, prices have got to be volatile if there's going to be a successful futures contract in the first place. If prices of cattle were rock-steady, neither ranchers nor meat-packers would need to hedge in the first place. In some markets, like oil, there are both organisations that try to hold prices steady, and active futures markets. The existence of a futures market usually means that the price-fixing organisation is not very successful.

So futures markets only exist where the price of the underlying commodity is volatile. And volatile prices mean high risk.

Margin

The second reason for the risky nature of investment in futures arises because of the rules of most of the futures markets. Most players in futures contracts do not have to put up the full price of the contracts which they buy and sell: instead, they operate on 'margin'. The margin is fixed as a low percentage of the total face value of the contracts being bought or sold.

You can immediately see why this will lead to volatility in the returns from investment. Suppose you buy a wheat contract for £100. However, instead of putting up the full £100 the margin requirement for this investment is only 15%; so it only costs £15 to get into the game. Now suppose that the price of the wheat rises so that the full value of the contract rises from £100 to £115.

That's a price change of only 15%, but your profit of £15 is equal to 100% of the amount of your initial stake.

Alternatively, if the price of the underlying wheat falls by 15% your initial investment is completely wiped out. Before this point is reached, however, futures exchange rules will require you to put in new money as fresh margin.

Just like companies with high amounts of debt, investors in futures markets are 'highly geared'. This means that a small percentage change in the value of the futures contracts that you own or owe can lead to an enormous change in your wealth. The table below gives some idea of the variability in the prices of some of the more important commodities. Many of the prices are much more volatile than those of shares. So you can see how an investor in margin in these commodities can easily face risks which are far greater than those to which he or she would be subjected in the share or bond markets. The rules of the market allow you to risk your shirt – indeed, if you have borrowed heavily, your entire wardrobe.

VARIABILITY OF COMMODITY PRICES

Coffee	192
Copper	132
Beef	120
Wheat	111
Shares	100
$/£ rate	77

(Note: quarterly variability of price changes over 10 years to 1988 3rd quarter, scaled so that shares = 100)

From soya beans to t-bonds ·

In the mid-1970s a revolution began to take place in the futures markets. The main Chicago exchanges, looking at the behaviour of some of the financial securities (for example, shares and bonds) which traders were buying and selling in New York and London, realised that many of them behaved in much the same way as commodities. They reasoned, 'If you can trade futures in soya beans, why can't you trade futures in Treasury bonds?'

They were right. You can. Today the Treasury Bond Futures market is the most successful and active pit at the Chicago Board of Trade. At its opening it looks like a section from Rodin's 'The Gates of Hell' – a huge mass of writhing arms as a swarm of dealers try to trade in the mighty T-Bond future.

The T-Bond is simply a bond, issued by the US Treasury, which pays you a fixed amount of interest over a period of 30 years and returns a capital amount at the end; it's an 'American gilt'. Bonds, as Chapter 3 explains, go up and down in value depending on movements in interest rates. This can make holders nervous: they're pleased to have a way to hedge their risk. The T-Bond future gives them the ability to buy or sell bonds at a fixed price at a future date. That is why, when the Board of Trade created the T-Bond futures, the market grew like Topsy.

Trading the index ·

With the success of the T-Bond future the futures exchanges grew more inventive. The Chicago Mercantile Exchange, deadly rivals to the Board of Trade despite their proximity, managed to get a market going in futures on the Standard and Poor's 500. This bit of creativity had some far-reaching and unforeseen consequences.

The Standard and Poor's 500 is a basket of the 500 shares which make up their index of American shares (see the section on 'indexes'). A futures market on the S and P 500 gives big investors the ability to hedge against movements in the entire stock market. It is very popular – and the pit is frenetic. However, just as is the case with wheat or cattle, the investor has the ability to buy or sell the underlying asset as well as the future. In this case the underlying 'asset' is the 500 shares in the index, in the same proportions as the index. This led big firms to set up computer systems which could do just that – buy or sell huge amounts of the 500 shares simultaneously. When index futures are 'cheap' against the underlying 500 shares, these large investors try to profit by buying futures and selling shares.

Such computer selling has been blamed by some people for contributing to the crash in the shares market on 19 October 1987. However, as with all crashes the reasons for the timing and scale of the 1987 crash will for ever remain a subject of inconclusive debate: as we saw in Chapter 4, there is good reason to believe that a major contributory factor was simply that share markets around the world had become overvalued.

Options ·

Options are futures with a twist. A futures contract gives you the right to take delivery of – or the obligation to provide – a specified amount of the commodity that you're interested in at a specified date in the future. If you own an option you have no obligation. An option gives you the right – but not the requirement – to buy or to sell a set amount of a commodity or a financial instrument at a specified price, on or before a specified date in the future.

Like futures contracts, options are available in standardised forms in organised markets (for example, the London Traded Options Market) on a wide range of underlying assets. You can trade in options on individual shares, share market indices, bonds and currencies. A 'call' option is the right to buy. A 'put' option is the right to sell. The price at which the option allows you to deal is its 'exercise' or 'strike' price. The date before which you can use an option is its 'expiration' date. Options are created between buyers and sellers just like futures contracts. Someone who sells an option 'writes' it.

Clearly, you'll only want to exercise an option which you own when it expires if it will be profitable to do so. Whoever sold you the option has no control over the situation – he or she can only hope that it won't be profitable to exercise. Suppose you own a call option. Exercising it will be profitable only if the actual price of the underlying asset (for example, a share) is above the 'exercise price' of your option. Options are like futures in the sense that they are highly-geared plays on the price performance of the underlying asset. The reason is that they cost only a fraction as much as the asset, but share fully in its price changes.

Consider a real-life example. At the time of writing, the price of Shell Transport shares is 362 pence; the price of a six-month option to buy Shell Transport shares at 390 pence is only 12 pence per share. All sorts of things can happen to the price of Shell shares over the course of six months. The option gives the owner the right to buy Shell shares at 390 pence. If the shares are trading at any level below 390 pence in six months' time this right will be worthless: anyone who wants to buy will be able to do so directly at lower cost. The whole of an investment in the options will have been wiped out.

It will make sense to exercise the option if the Shell price is above 390 pence. But the owner may still lose money. Suppose the Shell price in six months' time is 400 pence; the right to buy Shell shares at 390 pence will then be worth 10 pence. However, someone who bought this right for 12 pence will have lost $2 \div 12 = 17\%$ of his or her original investment. For the buyer of the call option just to break even, the Shell price must rise to 402 pence.

Suppose, however, that the price of Shell shares rises from 362 pence to 450 pence (a rise of about 24%). On expiration day the 390-pence call option will be worth 60 pence; the lucky buyer at 12 pence will have made a profit of 400%, quintupling his or her money. Huge returns – both positive and negative – can be achieved in options, even when the movement in the price of the underlying shares is much less dramatic.

The table on page 153 shows part of the *Financial Times*' daily report of the prices of options on shares currently available in the London Traded Options Market. There are a number of factors at work, some of which can be seen from the table.

For any one share, a call option will be more valuable:

1   the lower its exercise price is in relation to the price of the share;

2   the longer it has to run before expiration;

3   the more volatile is the price of the underlying share.

The first point is straightforward. Clearly, on expiration date, the only thing that matters for the value of a call option is the gap between the exercise price and the market price of the share. You'll pay more for the right to buy something for £10 than you'll pay for the right to buy it for £20. The share is more likely to reach £10 than soar to £20. (A call option is said to be 'in the money' when the price of the share is above the exercise price of the option.)

Options are more valuable the further they are from their expiration date. That requires a little more thought. The best way to put it is that share prices can go up or down, and the further ahead one's looking, the further the price is likely to be from the current level. What is important is that, the longer the option has to run, the greater is the chance that the price when the option expires will be a long way above today's price. The price of a Shell share tomorrow, or in a week's time, will be probably much the same as the price today. In a year's time who knows? It's the possibility of a big increase in the price that gives today's option its value. And the longer the life of the option, the more you'll have to pay for it.

The same principle applies to another feature of option pricing which isn't obvious from the table. This principle is that, the riskier and more volatile is the underlying share, the more valuable is the option to buy that share. A volatile share's price goes up and down violently. Remember, if you own a call option you are not obliged to exercise it, so the risk that the share might go down a long way needn't concern you. What gets into the price is the possibility – and it may be no more than that – that a volatile share will rise in price a long way. That makes an option on such a share correspondingly more valuable – and more expensive to buy.

Using options

This section might be called: don't use options. Be absolutely clear – except in some special circumstances which are discussed below, options are very risky investments. This is because their prices are extremely volatile – they can, and often do, swing wildly up and down. Options are not for you if you have any real concern about losing all of any sum that you have invested.

After the October 1987 share-market crash several cases came to light of people who had lost all that they had, and incurred debts for large amounts that they didn't have. In most cases these people had been playing the options markets. Sharp changes in prices can happen, even if they're infrequent. These changes have magnified effects on the value of options contracts – beware!

A defensive strategy

However, options can be used in a defensive, risk-reducing way. Farmers, with much of their wealth tied up in (say) wheat, can use futures contracts to hedge their risks. You can do much the same if you want to protect the value of an underlying investment (for example, in shares) on which options are

LONDON TRADED OPTIONS

Option	CALLS			PUTS		
	Jan	Apr	Jul	Jan	Apr	Jul
Allied Lyons (°467) 460	10	31	44	2½	13	22
500	1	12½	27	35	36	39
Brit. Airways (°175) 160	16	25	25	½	4	7
180	1	10	13	6	9	15
Brit. & Comm. (°230) 220	11	21	30	1	8	10
240	1½	11	16	12	17	19
B.P. (°268) 260	8½	13	21½	½	9	12
280	1	4¾	12½	11½	22½	24
British Steel (°70) 50	19¾	21½	23¼	¼	½	½
60	9¾	12½	13¾	¼	1	2½
70	1¼	5¼	7	1½	3½	6¾
Bass (°863) 850	18	52	82	4	23	32
900	2½	24	53	40	43	50
Cable & Wire (°396) 390	9	29	45	3	13	18
420	1	12	25	26	30	36
Cons. Gold (°1285) 1250	50	120	160	6	55	80
1300	12	85	125	20	80	110
1350	4	67	–	65	110	–
Courtaulds (°286) 280	8	23	31	2½	11	19
300	1½	13	21	15	22	29
Com. Union (°365) 360	10	16½	31	4	15	18
390	1	7	–	25	36	–
G.K.N. (°331) 330	4	17	28	4	17	20
360	½	5	15	30	39	43
Grand Met. (°472) 460	–	–	44	–	–	19
493	1	11	–	23	34	–
I.C.I. (°1072) 1050	25	52	78	3	28	33
1100	3	24	50	30	60	65
Jaguar (°278) 260	18	27	37	1	9	14
280	2½	13	24	5	18	22
300	1	6½	–	23	31	–
Land Securities (°579) 500	82	97	107	1	6	8
550	32	52	67	2	12	19
600	2	22	38	23	28	38
Marks & Spencer (°163) 140	24	29	31	½	1½	4
160	4	12½	16	1	5	9
180	¼	3½	6	18	18	19
STC (°295) 280	17	28	37	1½	9	14
300	3	16	26	7	17	22
Sainsbury (°215) 200	16	24	30	1	3½	7
220	1½	10	17	7	12	16
Shell Trans. (°362) 350	13	22	32	1	9	10
390	–	4	12	–	35	35
Storehouse (°189) 180	10	23	33	1	10	18
200	1½	13	22	14	20	27
1	–	–	–	–	–	–
Trafalgar House (°316) 280	37	45	52	1½	3	5
300	17	27	35	2	7	12
330	2	11	19	16	20	26

Option	
Plessey (°244)	200
	220
	240
Prudential (°171)	140
	160
	180
Racal (°323)	300
	330
	360
R.T.Z. (°478)	460
	500

Option	
Vaal Reefs (°$75)	70
	80

Option	
Amstrad (°164)	140
	160
	180
Barclays (°437)	390
	420
	460
Blue Circle (°470)	460
	500
Dixons (°139)	130
	140
Glaxo (°1111)	1100
	1150
Hawker Sidd. (°596)	500
	550
	600
Hillsdown (°260)	240
	260
Lonrho (°344)	330
	360
Midland Bk (°442)	420
	460
Sears (°117)	110
	120
Trusthouse Forte (°260)	240
	260
Thorn EMI (°685)	650
	700
Wellcome (°465)	460
	500
Option	

available. In this case your option involvement is 'covered' by your ownership of the underlying share.

Suppose you own a share which has gone up in price, but you're frightened that it may go down again. If you also buy a put option (the right to sell the share at a specified price), you will be insulated against the risk that the share goes down: if the share continues to rise you will get the profit from it; if, on the other hand, your fears are realised and the share falls in price, your put option will rise in value. Either way you are protected. However, this protection will cost you money – the initial cost of the put option which you have purchased. Remember also that the option will be more expensive, the longer is the period into the future that it covers. So you pay more for getting insurance for a longer period.

Another way of using options together with your existing investment in a share is to write a call option – that is, give someone else the right to buy the share from you at a pre-specified price. This means that you'll get money from the sale of the option up front, but that if the share soars in value you won't get any of the gains above the exercise price of the call. As your share soars in value, so will the value of the call you sold.

Aggressive strategies

A much more aggressive strategy using options is simply to buy them without owning the asset to which they relate. This is a 'naked' (as opposed to a covered) option strategy. You could either buy a call option, if you think the price of the underlying asset is going to rise, or a put option, if you think the price of the asset is going to fall.

As we saw in the Shell example, any such investment is highly geared. You may do much better than you would do by buying the underlying asset, or much worse. However, your maximum loss is limited to the amount of money you spend on the option. An option is never worth less than nothing! For this reason a naked option-buying strategy is less risky than the one that we'll talk about in the next paragraph.

The naked writer

The most aggressive use of options involves 'writing' them when you don't own the underlying security. This means that you give someone else the right to buy or sell something at a specified time at a specified price. You will, of course, receive the premium – the price of the option when you initially sell it. This may look like an easy way of making money. Remember, however, the risks involved.

Let's suppose that you write a put option on a share. That is, you're giving someone the right to sell you a share in a company at a specified price at some date in the future. If all goes well, the price of the share will rise, and no one will be interested in selling the share to you at the price you specified in your option. You will have the money from the initial sale of the option, and it will expire unused. However, suppose that for some reason the price of the share plunges. Remember, you have given someone else the right to sell that share to you at a specified price, probably close to the original price. You have taken on an almost open-ended liability. The amount of money you need to find may be very many times the amount of premium which you received.

Put out

Some investors got extremely badly burnt in the share-market crash of October 1987 because they had written put options on shares, or on the shares market as a whole. What had seemed an almost riskless and very profitable strategy during the great boom market – writing put options – suddenly proved to be no such thing. In the words of one options trader, 'the puts grew teeth'.

Accordingly, our advice to you on using such a strategy is simple: don't. Writing options (unless you are writing a call option on something you own already) is an extremely risky business. It should be left to the professionals.

Options on options

There are many more complicated options strategies, with exotic names, which lie beyond the scope of this book. (Some examples are 'bull spreads', 'range forwards', 'butterflies' and 'strangles'.) Some strategies effectively reduce total risk and potential return, while others add to it. In options, like other investments, there aren't many 'free lunches' around. So risk and potential return are normally closely related.

These complex options strategies are unlikely to be of interest to you unless you have very clear ideas about where a market is or isn't going. If you have such ideas congratulations – you certainly don't need this book. But it might be sensible to think about what would happen if you're not infallible . . .

Caveat emptor

Caveat emptor is a Latin phrase meaning 'let the buyer beware'. It's particularly appropriate if you're thinking of dealing in futures or options. There are risks in almost all investments – that's a major reason why they offer the returns that they do – but the risks in futures and options can be so large that they don't have a place in most small investors' portfolios. If, nevertheless, you do get involved, it may still be helpful to bear a few points in mind. Because of their potential for vast profit – and loss, futures and options dealing seems to attract rogues. Some investors have lost all their life savings by getting embroiled in highly speculative options trading, with very high commissions, with people who cold-called them. Never, ever, buy or sell shares or futures or options, through someone who has just phoned you up.

You should take care to make the first approaches yourself, and should take care only to approach reputable stockbrokers and other dealers. You should know the strategy you're following and why you're following it. You should be clear about exactly what it is that you're buying, and how its price may behave. You should also be clear as to the level of commission that you'll be paying. This is particularly important in the case of options. In many cases commission levels are based on the exercise price of the options. As we've seen, these are much higher than the prices you pay for the options themselves. So as a percentage of your initial stake commissions can be much higher in this form of investment.

Summary

Let's sum up on futures and options. Futures are contracts to buy and sell things – originally agricultural commodities, but now covering a wide range of different items, including financial securities – at some date in the future. Options are futures with a twist. The twist is that the owner of an option has the right, but no obligation, to make a purchase or sale. Both futures and options can be extremely risky investments. For this reason they generally have no place in the strategies of non-expert investors.

c h a p t e r · 8

Conclusions ·

Our tour of the major types of investment open to the private investor has revealed many specific things about them. There's no space here to restate all those points. However, the table below summarises the key characteristics of the different investments, one against another.

	Expected Return	Risk	Cost of dealing	Liquidity	Other
Property	Medium	Medium	High	Low	Best for house-'users'
Bank/Building Society accounts	Low	Low	Nil	Very high	Higher returns in 1980s
Government bonds	Medium	Medium	Low	Very high	Vulnerable to inflation
Index-linked bonds	Medium	Low/Med	Low	Very high	Inflation-proof
Shares	Med/high	High	High	High	Cut risk by diversification
Unit trusts	Med/high	Med/high	High	High	
Privatisations	High	High	Med/high	High	Check each issue closely
Futures/options	Variable	Can be very high	High	Medium	Handle with great care

The table should bring to mind the six steps to successful investment which were identified in Chapter 1.

To recap, they are:

1   Know yourself.

2   Consider all the options.

3   Be realistic.

4   Diversify.

5   Hunt for value.

6   Don't overtrade.

Our first principle is absolutely critical to making all the others work. Successful investment demands that you have a thorough knowledge of your own needs, responsibilities, desires and, last but not least, temperament. It's the combination of these things that determines how happy you'll be with any given investment strategy.

Be aware of the full range of different assets you might invest in. Many people have decided that they should keep all their money in the bank; or that property investment is the way to get rich; or that really successful investors go for 'penny' shares.

In fact, no one type of investment is likely to meet all your needs. Different assets have different characteristics. Some are more suitable for some people than for others. So it's important to get the big decision right: in general, what proportion of your money do you want to hold in each of the different types of investment? With luck, this book will have helped give you a better understanding of the main investment options available. (Where an investment hasn't been covered, it's a good idea to try to work out how it would fit into a table of the sort shown above.)

'Realism' is important, too. The table shows that you usually pay for higher returns in one way or another – high returns tend to go with high risk, or high dealing costs, or poor liquidity. There are very few free lunches around. You normally won't get something for nothing. The reason is, as we've seen, that the investment world is highly competitive. If you could get something for nothing other people would realise it too: they would bid up the price of the attractive asset, to the point where its return was once again in line with the risk that was involved in owning it. The exception proves the rule: under-priced privatisation issues are pretty close to something for nothing, because the price can't move until the shares are sold! That means that when some-one other than the government does offer you something for nothing, you ought to be very suspicious indeed. (Be careful about the government, too: remember BP!) If it's a fair offer, then it may well involve a degree of risk which you would personally find unacceptable. The other alternative, of course, is that the offer is a fraudulent one.

Another aspect of realism is that even 'high' real returns won't make a fortune for you overnight. For example, the average share has generated a real return averaging 7% per year since 1918: just fast enough to double your (inflation-adjusted) money every ten years.

One obvious way of cutting risk without damaging return is by diversification. This means both owning different types of investment, and different items of the same type – especially shares. Unless you know a great deal about the strength of a particular basket – and you almost certainly don't – you shouldn't put all your eggs in it.

The first four steps listed above can be seen as the route to a successful investment strategy. They'll affect, for example, how much of your money you'll normally want to hold in shares as opposed to cash. The last two steps – hunting for value, and not over-trading – are as important, but can be seen as a good guide to investment 'tactics'. They help to answer questions like: should I buy share A or share B; or, is now a good time to move to a larger house?

In the end, of course, no book can make your investment decisions for you. Only you can do that. There's no substitute for staying alert and well-informed if you want to make money make money.

*G*lossary ·

This section explains terms commonly used in the financial markets. In many cases the terms are also defined in the main text.

Acquisition   This is what happens when one company buys another. Shareholders of the old company are given either cash, or shares in the acquiring company, as compensation. It's the same as a takeover.

Alpha   The highly liquid shares of the 100 or so largest UK companies are referred to as 'alpha' shares. Alphas are normally cheaper to deal in and less risky – although less exciting – than the shares of smaller companies, which are listed as 'betas, gammas or deltas'.

Annual general meeting   The meeting, required by law, where the Chairman and Directors of a company give a report of the year's activities to shareholders. Shareholders also have the right to raise any other business at the AGM.

Arbitrage   Where investors buy something cheaply in one market, in order to sell it for more money in another. For example, arbitrage ensures that the shares of the same company, quoted in different countries, trade at the same price. 'Arbitrageurs', who make a living by arbitrage, rarely hold shares for more than a very short time. Not recommended for the small investor.

Asset   Something of value which an investor or a company owns. Thus, for an investor, shares, bonds and cash are all assets. For a company, assets include physical assets – like factories, or stocks of materials – as well as financial assets.

Bear   A bear believes that a market is going to fall. Investors who are 'bearish' will not invest in the thing that they are pessimistic about. If they are aggressively bearish they may attempt to sell it short – sell the asset that they do not own, in the hope of buying it back later on more cheaply. The opposite of a bear is a bull.

Beta   The second tier of shares traded in the London Stock Exchange. These are fairly liquid, but less so than the hundred largest shares which are classed as alpha shares. Confusingly, the mathematically-minded also use beta to measure the sensitivity of a share to the general movement in share prices. A company with a high beta will tend to go up more than the market when the market is rising, but to fall more rapidly when the market is falling. High beta shares are attractive to investors who believe that the market will rise. Low beta shares are more suitable for a defensive investor.

Bid price   The amount a market-maker will pay you for a security (share, bond, or option).

Blue chip   A large and secure company.

Bond   Originally an American term meaning a bundle of debt on which interest is paid – which could be issued by companies or governments. Now 'bond' has become a generic term, both in the UK and US, for simply 'debt on which interest is paid'. For purists the proper word for 'bonds' is 'stock' – but probably only Victorians, or Bank of England officials, would recognise the distinction now.

Book value   The value of a company to shareholders, as carried in its books or accounts. Also known as net assets. Book value per share is the value of the company to shareholders divided by the number of shares outstanding. Book value can be an indicator of a company's underlying worth.

Bull   The opposite to a bear. A bull believes that a market is going to rise. Therefore he will be heavily invested in it, and perhaps take a very aggressive stance towards it.

Call   One sort of option. The right, but not the obligation, to buy something at a specified price at a future date. The owner of a call option on an asset believes that the asset will rise in price. If it does rise in price the owner of a call may make a large profit. On the other hand, if the expected price rise does not occur the call expires worthless: the owner will then have lost all of the money that he initially put into it.

Capital appreciation   A rise in the price of something. The owners of most investments hope to benefit from both capital appreciation and income.

Capital asset pricing model   Usually abbreviated to CAPM. An academic model of asset prices, which states that every asset is priced so that it gives an expected return which is in line with its (unavoidable) risk. The model is hard to test, but the general idea that risk and return are related is well documented.

Capitalisation   The total market value of an asset or company. A stream of cash flows (e.g. what a company generates) is said to be 'capitalised' when a price is put on them.

Cash flow   The amount of money which a company is generating before account is taken of depreciation. In other words, it is the amount that you could take out of a company if you weren't at all concerned about keeping it going. Cash flow per share is total cash flow divided by the number of shares outstanding.

Chartism   The belief that, just by studying charts of the past price movement of a share or asset, you can tell what the next move is going to be. Known as an 'ism' because it is, to its enthusiasts, akin to a religion. It also requires faith: there is no evidence at all that it leads to superior investment results.

Coupon   What a bond pays out on a regular basis, usually once or twice a year. It is a fixed-interest payment.

Depreciation   The allowance made in company accounts for the wearing away of buildings and equipment. Most companies use 'historic cost' depreciation, which can greatly understate the amount of money they will need to spend on replacing a piece of equipment when it finally does wear out completely. Depreciation is the difference between cash flow and earnings.

Dilution   What happens when a company, in issuing more shares, reduces the share of earnings attributable to the original holders. The value of their holdings is said to be diluted.

Diversification   Not putting all one's eggs in one basket. Investors can diversify by putting some money into each of several different types of asset, and also by splitting up the money they do put into one asset amongst several different securities. A good way of reducing risk.

Dividend   The cash that a company pays out to its shareholders on a regular basis, usually once or twice a year.

Dividend discount model   The model which values share prices by discounting all expected future dividends from those shares. The 'rational' way of valuing a share.

Dividend yield   The year's dividend from a share, expressed as a percentage of the share price.

Earnings   The after-tax profits of a company. Earnings per share are total earnings divided by the number of shares outstanding. Earnings are keenly watched by investors and analysts – they are the measure of the profitability of a company, and hence of what can be expected by way of current and future dividends.

Earnings yield   Earnings per share as a percentage of the share price.

Efficient markets theory   A theory that states that all information relevant to the price of a share is already embodied in that price. Efficient markets theory implies that you cannot use publicly-available information to predict where a share will go. You are as likely to pick a successful portfolio by throwing darts at a dart-board with the *Financial Times* shares page on it, as you are through deep research; anything that deep research can do is already embodied in share prices. While the efficient markets theory probably isn't absolutely true, it's a very good way of testing your thinking about investment ideas.

Equity   Another word for shares.

Eurobond   A bond issued in the 'Euro markets', outside the country in which the currency or bond is native. That means that it's independent of any particular national market, and so independent of regulation. Eurobonds come in all currencies: so there's Euro-sterling, Euro-dollars, Euro-yen, Euro-guilders, and so on.

Flotation   What happens when a company is launched on the share market. A flotation means selling shares to the general public. Most of the privatisation issues launched by the government involved fresh flotations.

Future   A contract entitling the owner to take delivery of something at a specified date in the future. Futures can be very volatile investments, both because the prices of the underlying assets are volatile and because of the low percentage of the final contract which is required when buying them. They originally arose in commodities markets, but have now extended to most financial markets.

Gearing   The extent to which a company has borrowed against its assets. A highly-geared company has a high ratio of debt (bank loans or bonds) to equity. This usually means that its profits are highly volatile. When times are bad there may not be enough money to pay the large interest required on the debt; when times are good profits expand dramatically relative to the very small share base.

Gilts   Gilts, or gilt-edged securities, are bonds issued by the British government. They are so called because they are as 'good as gold'; there is no risk that they will not be repaid.

Historic cost   The convention used in most company accounts. It means that assets are valued at what it cost to buy them originally: which may bear no resemblance to what they would cost to replace now!

Index   A way of measuring the performance of something, especially the shares market (for example, the FT–SE 100-share Index). The Retail Price Index measures the general level of prices.

Index-linked   An investment which is in some way tied to the Retail Price Index, and so is 'inflation-proof'. Available in some gilts and some National Savings investments.

Interest   The regular payment per period which an investor in building society or bank accounts, or other fixed-interest securities, gets for putting money into these assets.

Interim   An interim dividend is one that is paid in respect of earnings before the full year's results are known. It is typically paid on the basis of the first half of the earnings for that financial year. It gives shareholders more rapid access to their dividends, and some idea of what the total dividend for the year will be.

Junk bond   A bond which offers a very high yield, because repayments are uncertain. Junk bonds are issued by companies with unstable results or a very high level of debt. In the United States, junk bonds have been used extensively to finance takeovers by companies which could not or did not want to raise money in any other way. Not recommended as an investment for the private or any non-expert investor.

Liability   Something which a person or company owes. This is the opposite of an asset. For example, an individual's mortgage is a liability. Because company balance sheets, by convention, balance, assets must equal liabilities. As a result, liabilities in a company's accounts include not only bank loans, bond issues and the like, but also the notional amount owed to shareholders. Hence the surprising finding that share capital, and reserves owed to shareholders, count as liabilities.

Liquidity   This measures the speed and ease with which an asset can be turned into cash. Some assets are much more liquid than others. Money in a bank current account is a good example of a highly liquid asset. Shares are less liquid. Property is extremely illiquid.

In the context of a whole economy, liquidity refers to the amount of cash available in the system relative to the need for it. The buoyancy of the Japanese equity market has on occasion been interpreted as due to the high level of liquidity in the Japanese economy.

Margin   The fraction of the underlying value of a security that the investor has to put down in order to purchase it. The low margins required is one of the reasons why investment in futures is so risky.

Market-maker   Someone who stands ready to buy or sell, and so makes a market, in shares or bonds. The market-maker (usually a subsidiary of a large financial institution) holds an inventory of shares, and is willing to buy or sell at the (different!) prices which he announces.

The multiple   See *Price-earnings ratio*.

Nominal   The nominal return on an investment is the rate of profit on it, expressed in everyday money terms. Contrasts with the real return, which adjusts for inflation.

Offer   The higher of the two prices announced by a market-maker. That is, the offer price is the price at which the market-maker is prepared to sell securities to an investor.

Option   The right but not the obligation to deal in a security at a specified price sometime in the future. An option to buy is called a call; an option to sell, a put.

Payout ratio   The share of a company's earnings paid out to shareholders as dividends.

Price-earnings ratio   The price of a share, divided by the company's after-tax earnings (profits) due to that share over the most recent year. Sometimes the ratio is calculated using expected rather than historical earnings. Often shortened to P/E ratio, and also known as 'the multiple', this is the single most-used indicator of underlying share value. A high price-earnings ratio shows that investors are willing to pay a lot for a given amount of this year's earnings by a company, probably because they expect earnings to grow rapidly in future. A low P/E ratio means that the investor is getting the earnings 'cheaply': it implies lack of confidence that earnings will grow quickly.

Privatisation   The selling of previously state-owned companies into the private sector. Much practised by the Conservative government in the 1980s. The prices at which shares in the companies were offered were often too good to miss.

Put   An option which gives the right to sell something at some specified date in the future at a specified price. An investor who is pessimistic about the price of a share might buy a put option on it; this would give the right to sell the share at a pre-specified price, even if the actual price goes lower. The opposite to a put is a call.

Rating   This is used in two distinct senses. The rating of a share normally means its price-earnings ratio. The rating of an individual share can be compared with the rating of the market as a whole, or the rating of the share's business sector.

The other use of rating is by those who try to measure the credit quality of bonds. Thus a triple-A rating (the best) shows that analysts believe that there is very little risk associated with the bonds. A poor rating means a significant risk that the money the investor puts into bonds will not be repaid. Thus junk bonds carry relatively low ratings.

Rationalisation   Cost-cutting. Companies which are rationalising are normally in trouble.

Real estate   An American term for what the British call 'property'. But beware – the Americans define 'property' as everything an individual or company owns, not merely houses or buildings. Strictly speaking, the Americans are right!

Real return   The rate of profit on an investment after allowing for inflation. If a rate of return in nominal or money terms is 5% per year but inflation is running at 3% per year, the real return is only about 2% per year. If you're interested in what your investment can buy, you care about real rather than nominal returns.

Return   The rate of profit on an investment, normally expressed as a rate per year. So if a share goes up in price from £2 to £2.20 over two years, the total return is 10%; the rate of return is about 5% per year. Returns are usually quoted in simple money ('nominal') terms; it's also worth knowing what the real (adjusted-for-inflation) return has been.

Rights issue   The way a company raises more money by issuing more shares. Existing shareholders get the chance to buy more shares at a cheap price. However, it normally means that the value of their existing shares goes down. For this reason, rights issues are not popular with investors. They normally expect to get money back from a company; with a rights issue the company is taking money away from them.

Risk   What almost all investors are trying to avoid. The level of risk varies greatly from one investment to another. There are two important points to be made about risk. The first is that diversification – across different types of asset, and different shares or properties – can considerably reduce risk. The second is that what's risky for you depends on your own plans and needs. If you want a set sum of money in a year's time, your idea of what is risky will be very different from that of a person who plans to pay private school fees in ten years' time. So be careful not to take statements about riskiness at face value.

Risk aversion   The degree to which people dislike risk. It obviously varies from individual to individual. In general, richer people are less risk averse. They are less worried about losing money because they already have lots of it.

Share   The title to ownership of a part (usually a very small part) of a company. The owners of shares in a company are the owners of that company.

Stag   Someone who buys a new issue of shares in hopes of making an instant profit from them. Many small investors became aggressive stags in the privatisations of the mid-1980s. While 'stagging' some of these issues was an almost-guaranteed way to success, stagging in general is a relatively high-risk way of investing.

Stock   The original name for a bond (see 'Bonds'). Confusingly, Americans refer to shares as stocks.

Synergy   The notion that the whole is greater than the sum of its parts. Synergy is often invoked by managers of companies who are involved in a bold programme of takeovers. The idea is that a dry-cleaning company and an oil company naturally do better when they are part of the same organisation. It's a notion that you should always treat with great scepticism.

Takeover   The same as an acquisition. There is a tendency for companies to take over other companies when they have a lot of cash and nothing more creative to spend it on. Most takeovers do little or nothing for the shareholders of the company doing the buying: the people who do well are the managers of the buying company (who get a bigger empire to run) and the shareholders of the company that gets bought.

Technical analysis   Another name for chartism.

Undated bonds   Examples of this are Consols or War Loan. These pay a coupon regularly, but will be redeemed at the option of the government – probably never. See Bonds.

Value   The underlying worth of an asset. Hard-line believers in the Efficient Markets Theory think that the value of a share is always equal to its price. Certainly the two are often difficult to tell apart. However, the evidence suggests that the most successful long-term investors are those who do hunt for value.

Volume   The amount of trading going on in a company's shares. This is usually measured in terms of number of shares traded in a day, or a week.

Yield   This can be either earnings yield or dividend yield. In either case it measures the amount in question as a percentage of the value of the share. So a company with a share price of 200 pence which pays a dividend of 10 pence a year is said to have a dividend yield of 5%.

*I*ndex ·

Acknowledgements ·

Without Alan Haydn Griffiths, the producer of the BBC television programmes 'Make Money Make Money', neither the series nor this book would exist. He is responsible for the original idea, persuaded me to write the book, and unfailingly encouraged me while I was at work on it. My debt to him is far greater than is acknowledged by his status as editor of the book.

Guy Jillings of Shell International has long stimulated my thinking about investment issues. My colleagues at First Chicago Investment Advisors, particularly Tony Robinson, Susan Hakki-Haroun, Suzanne Phillips, and Ronald Aziz, also get much of whatever credit this book deserves. They have consciously or unconsciously acted as expert critics on several sections. However, neither they nor First Chicago Investment Advisors are responsible for the final product!

Joanna Hase typed the first drafts quickly and accurately. Alix Harrower designed the book, and Martin Soames provided some of the publicity material. Suzanne Webber and (especially) Julian Flanders of BBC Books got the book from manuscript to publication. My thanks to all of them, and to Charles Peattie and Russell Taylor for permitting the use of some of their 'Alex' cartoons (courtesy of Penguin Books and the Kingswood Press).

The families of all authors bear a load: the families of part-time authors bear a particularly heavy load. To Dorcas and Edward my thanks for their forbearance, and the promise that I won't write another one (just yet . . .).